THE GREAT LIEDER CYCLES
IN ENGLISH SINGING TRANSLATIONS

THE GREAT LIEDER CYCLES

IN ENGLISH SINGING TRANSLATIONS

Jeffrey Benton

Copyright © 2023 Jeffrey Benton
Translations copyright of Jeffrey Benton
www.jeffreybenton.co.uk

The moral right of the author has been asserted.

Apart from any fair dealing for the purposes of research or private study, or criticism or review, as permitted under the Copyright, Designs and Patents Act 1988, this publication may only be reproduced, stored or transmitted, in any form or by any means, with the prior permission in writing of the publishers, or in the case of reprographic reproduction in accordance with the terms of licences issued by the Copyright Licensing Agency. Enquiries concerning reproduction outside those terms should be sent to the publishers.

Matador
Unit E2 Airfield Business Park,
Harrison Road, Market Harborough,
Leicestershire. LE16 7UL
Tel: 0116 2792299
Email: books@troubador.co.uk
Web: www.troubador.co.uk/matador
Twitter: @matadorbooks

ISBN 978 1805141 433

British Library Cataloguing in Publication Data.
A catalogue record for this book is available from the British Library.

Printed and bound by CPI Group (UK) Ltd, Croydon, CR0 4YY
Typeset in 12pt Adobe Jenson Pro by Troubador Publishing Ltd, Leicester, UK

Matador is an imprint of Troubador Publishing Ltd

*For Dorothy,
My Own Beloved.*

*And To Mario Lanza
For The Eternal Inspiration.*

"Music and Poetry have ever been acknowledged Sisters,
which walking hand in hand support each other;
As poetry is the harmony of words, so music is that of notes;
and as poetry is a rise above prose and oratory, so is music
the exaltation of poetry.
Both of them may excel apart, but sure they are most
excellent when they are joined, because nothing is then
wanting to either of their perfections."

Henry Purcell 1659 – 1695

Here, for the first time, a singer has created a true, line by line, translation of all the song cycles of Schubert and Schumann, along with Beethoven's *An die ferne Geliebte* (To The Distant Beloved), Mahler's *Lieder eines fahrenden Gesellen* (Songs Of A Wayfarer) and the rare *Eliland* by Alexander Von Fielitz.

"With the needs of the singer, and also the listener in mind, I have by each line a faithful, rhyming translation of the original poems.

It became clear to me at the start of my concert career, at my very first recital at London's Wigmore Hall, that the greater part of the audience were hearing only piano and voice, and that the wonderful poetry which was the inspiration of the composer, was lost to the listener.

My ambition was to translate and make recordings of all the great song cycles so that the whole world can enjoy the wonderful poetry set to music".

Jeffrey Benton

Foreword

Jeffrey Benton has achieved that which no other has done. He has convinced me that songs in German can and ought to be performed in English. These translations demonstrate that merely the German sound is absent.

That which no one before him has done, Jeffrey has accomplished in ensuring that these songs may also be embraced in English. Not only has he translated all of these cycles, in itself an incredible achievement, making use of his profound knowledge of what is singable, he has also performed all but one (Schwanengesang) on many occasions, and recorded them too.

He has even made me love the Beethoven and Mahler cycles more than I do in German.

Where previously compromises have been considered inevitable in translations of the past, there are none made here. Poetry is often sacrificed for directness, but a lifetime's work of revision, improvement and adjustment has shown that this sacrifice can be overcome.

I don't have, cannot have quite the same emotional response to the words when sung in the original German, no matter how fluent I may be, forging an emotional connection to the words I hear and sing can be done most truthfully and powerfully in my own language.

It helps me connect to the emotional journey of the poets' story and the composers' music on a fundamental level.

Jeffrey's skill in these translations, in my view, is in his refusal to compromise fidelity to the poets' exact text, and a desire to have the English flow naturally. He has also found words and sentence structures that fit the shapes of each composer's melodies and I think this is where he has been so successful. It occurs to me that had Schubert, Schumann, Mahler, Beethoven and Von Fielitz been given these lyrics, they might easily have composed for them the melodies that we already know.

The collection of these important song cycles for this book is invaluable and should be included in the library of all lovers of Art-Song and Lieder.

Derek Hammond-Stroud OBE

Contents

1/ **To The Distant Beloved** (An die ferne Geliebte)   1
Ludwig Van Beethoven (Alois Jeitteles)

2/ **The Fair Maiden Of The Mill** (Die schöne Müllerin)   9
Franz Schubert (Wilhelm Müller)

3/ **The Winter Journey** (Winterreise)   43
Franz Schubert (Wilhelm Müller)

4/ **Swan Song** (Schwanengesang)   72
Franz Schubert (Ludwig Rellstab, 7 Poems)
(Heinrich Heine, 6 Poems)
(Johann Seidl, 1 Poem)

5/ **A Poet's Love** (Dichterliebe)   91
Robert Schumann (Heinrich Heine)

6/ **Song Cycle** (Liederkreis) Op 24   109
Robert Schumann (Heinrich Heine)

7/ **Song Cycle** Op 35   120
Robert Schumann (Justinus Kerner)

8/ **Song Cycle** (Liederkreis) Op 39   135
     Robert Schumann (Josepf von Eichendorff)

9/ **A Woman's Love And Life** (Frauen-Liebe und Leben)   148
     Robert Schumann (Adelbert von Chamisso)

10/ **Songs Of A Wayfarer** (Lieder eines fahrenden Gesellen)   158
     Gustav Mahler (Gustav Mahler)

11/ **Eliland – Song Of Chiemsee** (Ein Sang Von Chiemsee)   164
     Alexander von Fielitz (Kaspar Stieler)

Ludwig Van Beethoven

An die ferne Geliebte – To The Distant Beloved

With this song-cycle Beethoven made a significant formal contribution to the literature of German art-song. When he set the six poems of Alois Jeitteles he created the form: Liederkreis, as he called it. This duo-sonata for voice and piano was revolutionary in that the poems are linked by transitional piano passages which hold the attention throughout.

This continuity, however, was not adopted by any of the major song-composers. The unceremonious modulations of rhythm, tonality and tempo in the first three songs are beautifully formed. For example, the melodic line of the first is shaped in such a manner that it would be appropriate to all five verses. In the following song the bold treatment of the second stanza in which the singer muses abstractedly on a single note as to "where he would rather be" is wonderfully inventive. The final song incorporates the evocative opening theme relating to nature and the joys of youth. Schumann was so taken by the work that he wove the melody of the sixth song into the first movement of his *C major Fantaisie* which he dedicated to Clara Wieck.

© Philip Rodden

1.

Auf dem Hügel sitz ich spähend
In das blaue Nebelland,
Nach den fernen Triften sehend,
Wo ich dich, Geliebte, fand.

Weit bin ich von dir geschieden,
Trennend liegen Berg und Tal
Zwischen uns und unserm Frieden,
Unserm Glück und unsrer Qual.

Ach, den Blick kannst du nicht sehen,
Der zu dir so glühend eilt,
Und die Seufzer, sie verwehen
In dem Raume, der uns teilt.

Will denn nichts mehr zu dir dringen,
Nichts der Liebe Bote sein?
Singen will ich, Lieder singen,
Die dir klagen meine Pein!

Denn vor Liebesklang entweichet
Jeder Raum und jede Zeit,
Und ein liebend Herz erreichet
Was ein liebend Herz geweiht!

1.

On a hillside I sit gazing
at the blue and hazy land,
thinking of the distant meadows,
where we wandered hand in hand

Now so far from you beloved,
hills and valleys lie between
us and our devotion,
and our joys and all our pain.

Ah, you cannot see the longing,
which is burning in my eyes,
and my sighs are widely scattered
in the space that between us lies.

Then will nothing ever reach you,
can loves messenger not say?
Will you hear my songs lamenting,
songs of anguish and dismay!

And yet time and distance vanish
to the strains of lover's songs,
and a loving heart can reach out
where a loving heart belongs.

2.

Wo die Berge so blau
Aus dem nebligen Grau
Schauen herein,
Wo die Sonne verglüht,
Wo die Wolke umzieht,
Möchte ich sein!
Möchte ich sein!

Dort im ruhigen Tal
Schweigen Schmerzen und Qual.
Wo im Gestein
Still die Primel dort sinnt,
Weht so leise der Wind,
Möchte ich sein!
Möchte ich sein!

Hin zum sinnigen Wald
Drängt mich Liebesgewalt,
Innere Pein,
Innere Pein.

Ach, mich zög's nicht von hier,
Könnt ich, Traute, bei dir
Ewiglich sein!
Ewiglich sein!

2.

Where the mountains so blue
from the grey mists arise,
that's what I see.
Where the sun fades from view,
where the clouds sail the skies,
there I would be!
there I would be!

In the valley of peace
pain and sorrow will cease,
and in the rocks
silent primroses know,
where the soft breezes blow,
there would I go!
there would I go!

To the dark brooding wood,
urged by love's violent mood
feeling my pain,
feeling my pain.

Ah! it's here I would bide,
if she were by my side,
mine to remain!
mine to remain!

3.

Leichte Segler in den Höhen,
Und du, Bächlein klein und schmal,
Könnt mein Liebchen ihr erspähen,
Grüßt sie mir viel tausendmal.

Seht ihr, Wolken, sie dann gehen
Sinnend in dem stillen Tal,
Laßt mein Bild vor ihr entstehen
In dem luft'gen Himmelssaal.

Wird sie an den Büschen stehen,
Die nun herbstlich falb und kahl.
Klagt ihr, wie mir ist geschehen,
Klagt ihr, Vöglein, meine Qual.

Stille Weste, bringt im Wehen
Hin zu meiner Herzenswahl
Meine Seufzer, die vergehen
Wie der Sonne letzter Strahl.

Flüstr' ihr zu mein Liebesflehen,
Laß sie, Bächlein klein und schmal,
Treu in deinen Wogen sehen
Meine Tränen ohne Zahl!
ohne Zahl!

3.

Light clouds sailing in the heavens,
little streamlet fast and free,
greet my sweetheart if you see her,
many thousand times from me.

Then o clouds, if you should see her,
walking sadly in the vale,
let my image rise before her
in the air through which you sail.

If you see her in the garden,
now that Autumn pales the leaves,
tell her little birds my troubles,
tell her how my heart still grieves.

Calm west wind bring on your breezes,
send them to my heart's desire,
and my sighing soon will vanish
like the sunset's dying fire.

Whisper all my love beseeching
little streamlet as you go,
and upon your rippling surface,
countless tears to her will flow,
Countless tears.

4.

Diese Wolken in den Höhen,
Dieser Vöglein muntrer Zug,
Werden dich, o Huldin, sehen.
Nehmt mich mit im leichten Flug!

Diese Weste werden spielen
Scherzend dir um Wang' und Brust,
In den seidnen Locken wühlen.
Teilt ich mit euch diese Lust!

Hin zu dir von jenen Hügeln
Emsig dieses Bächlein eilt.
Wird ihr Bild sich in dir spiegeln,
Fließ zurück dann unverweilt!
Fließ zurück dann unverweilt!
Ja unverweilt!

4.

All the clouds on high above me,
merry birds that fill the sky,
if you see my gracious dear one,
take me with you as you fly.

Oh west wind so gladly playing
round her cheeks and breasts divine
in her silken hair to nestle,
could such joy be also mine.

From the hills the busy stream
is flowing quickly on its way,
should you catch her sweet reflection,
flow back here without delay,
flow back here without delay,
without delay.

5.

Es kehret der Maien,
Es blühet die Au,
Die Lüfte, sie wehen
So milde, so lau,
Geschwätzig die Bäche nun rinnen.

Die Schwalbe, die kehret
Zum wirtlichen Dach,
Sie baut sich so emsig
Ihr bräutlich Gemach,
Die Liebe soll wohnen da drinnen,
Die Liebe soll wohnen da drinnen.

Sie bringt sich geschäftig
Von kreuz und von Quer
Manch weicheres Stück
Zu dem Brautbett hieher,
Manch wärmendes Stück für die Kleinen.

Nun wohnen die Gatten
Beisammen so treu,
Was Winter geschieden,
Verband nun der Mai,
Was liebet, das weiß er zu einen,
Was liebet, das weiß er zu einen.

Es kehret der Maien,
Es blühet die Au.
Die Lüfte, sie wehen
So milde, so lau;
Nur ich kann nicht ziehen von hinnen.

Wenn alles, was liebet,
Der Frühling vereint,
Nur unserer Liebe
Kein Frühling erscheint,
Und Tränen sind all ihr Gewinnen,
Und Tränen sind all ihr Gewinnen,
Ja all ihr Gewinnen.

5.

The Maytime is here
with the meadows in bloom,
the mild breezes blow
with a fragrant perfume,
and babbling the streamlets are flowing.

The swallow returns
to the roof she knows best,
and eagerly fashions
the soft bridle nest,
for there shall love be dwelling,
for there shall love be dwelling.

They criss-cross the sky
as they fly overhead
to gather soft down
for a new bridal bed,
to give needed warmth for the young ones.

She's paired to her mate
In a faithful display,
what winter divided
is joined now by May,
as all things by love are united,
as all things by love are united.

The Maytime is here
with the meadows in bloom,
the mild breezes blow
with a fragrant perfume.
Why then do I have to remain here?

When Spring has united
the faithful and true,
then why has the Spring
not returned me to you,
rewarding us only with weeping,
rewarding us only with weeping,
yes only with weeping.

6.

Nimm sie hin denn, diese Lieder,
Die ich dir, Geliebte, sang,
Singe sie dann abends wieder
Zu der Laute süßem Klang!

Wenn das Dämmrungsrot dann ziehet
Nach dem stillen blauen See,
Und sein letzter Strahl verglühet
Hinter jener Bergeshöh;

Und du singst, und du singst,
was ich gesungen,
Was mir aus der vollen Brust
Ohne Kunstgepräng erklungen,
Nur der Sehnsucht sich bewußt,
Nur, nur der Sehnsucht sich bewußt:

Dann vor diesen Liedern weichet
Was geschieden uns so weit,
Und ein liebend Herz erreichet
Was ein liebend Herz geweiht!
Und ein liebend Herz erreichet
Was ein liebend, ein liebend,
Ein liebend Herz geweiht.

Dann, dann vor diesen Liedern weichet,
Was geschieden uns so weit,
Und ein liebend Herz erreichet,
Was ein liebend Herz,
Ein liebend Herz geweiht,
Was, was ein liebend,
Liebend Herz geweiht!

6.

Take then, take these songs I'm singing,
share in them the love I found,
sing them in the quiet evening
to the lute's sweet sound.

When the twilight glow has faded
on the lake so blue, so still.
As its last dim rays are shaded,
as it sinks behind the hill.

And you sing, and you sing
the songs I'm singing,
from a full and simple heart,
from a heart that knows such longing,
conscious only of its love.
Love, only longing, only love.

Then before us all Is yielding
to the sound of lover's songs,
and a loving heart can reach out
where a loving heart belongs,
and a loving heart can reach out
where a loving heart, my heart,
where a loving heart belongs.

Then, then all yields to our devotion,
to the sound of lover's songs,
and a loving heart can reach out
to a loving heart,
to where a heart belongs.
Where, where a loving,
loving heart belongs.

Franz Schubert

Die schöne Müllerin – The Fair Maiden of the Mill

By sheer weight of their numbers (over 600) the songs of Schubert occupy a disproportionately large position in the repertory of the high romantic lied. Following the publication of Beethoven's *An die ferne Geliebte*, the idea of a song cycle began to interest Schubert. But it wasn't until he came across the poems of Wilhelm Müller in the spring of 1823 that he decided to set some of them to music, which he perpetuated by his compositional genius.

He began work on *Die schöne Müllerin* in the summer of 1823, and completed the cycle in November that year which he dedicated to Karl Freiherr von Schonstein.

Schubert and Vogl, a leading light of the Vienna court opera, performed some of the songs in Linz on 28th July 1823. It seems incredible that the cycle was not presented in its entirety until Julius Stockhausen performed it in Vienna on 6th May 1856, thirty-two years after it was first published and twenty-eight years after Schubert's death. It would be folly to state that Müller's lyrics were of the same merit as those of Heine, Goethe, Eichendorf, or the influential Swabian Eduard Morike. Nevertheless, we are indebted to Müller for inspiring Schubert to string together a garland of exquisite melodies.

Müller, certainly with an awareness of the pun on his own name (Das Wandern ist des Müllers Lust) in the opening song, accounts in this transparent poem for the young miller's fondness for roving. The main means of communication here is the music of the water, which is used to connect each of the stanzas. A syllabic text setting with emphasis on the repetition of the most significant words 'Wandering', 'Water', and 'Millstones' provide an element of folksiness. Not only do the words fall on the first note, or accented beat of the measure, they keep everything in harness. In the following song, 'Whither?', the brook is released from the millwheel, and meanders at its own sweet will. The song is in the form of a question. There are two implications here: where will the brook lead the youth? Should he follow it? What then will be his destiny? At the phrase 'Downward will I follow the stream' Schubert uses the bass clef to deepen the current.

In the most beautiful song of the cycle, 'The Inquirer', he asks the brook if the maid loves him, his whole world is contained in the brook's reply, will it be yes or no? Here Schubert uses recitative in an effortless fashion. The transition from B major at the phrase 'yes is the word I hope for' through C major to G major, demonstrates the composer's skill at giving depth and perspective to the lied. The story of 'Mine' is short and uncomplicated, the proverbial love-bug has done excellent work on the boy's behalf as he exuberantly sings 'The maid of the mill is mine!' Here we encounter the first fortissimos in the cycle. The introduction also serves as a postlude, and what a delightful end it makes.

The horn call in the C minor song 'The Hunter', with its few bars of scherzo accents, announces the arrival of the huntsman upon the scene. The miller sees him as a rival for the affections of his loved one and voices his anger in tones bristling with resentment. In the penultimate song 'The Miller and the Brook', the dialogue between the miller and his only friend, the brook, is moving to a degree. With the gentlest ripple of semiquavers the brook sings its song of comfort, here is a beautiful modulation from B flat at the words 'a cooling peace' to G major at 'Dearest streamlet sing on and never cease'.

In the final E major song, 'The Brook's Lullaby', the gentle rocking effect at the phrase 'till the stream is embraced by the ocean' is felicity itself.

In conclusion. I leave the final words to Johann Michael Vogl the great interpreter, and champion of Schubert-Lieder.

"Nothing shows so plainly the want of a good school of singing as Schubert's songs…how many would have comprehended, probably for the first time, the meaning of such expressions as 'speech in music.' 'words in harmony.' 'ideas clothed in music,' and so forth, and would have learnt that the finest poems of our greatest poets may be enhanced and even transcended when translated into musical language?"

© Philip Rodden

1. Das Wandern

Das Wandern ist des Müllers Lust,
Das Wandern!
Das Wandern ist des Müllers Lust,
Das Wandern!
Das muss ein schlechter Müller sein,
Dem niemals fiel das Wandern ein,
Das Wandern, das Wandern,
Das Wandern, das Wandern.

Vom Wasser haben wir's gelernt,
Vom Wasser!
Vom Wasser haben wir's gelernt,
Vom Wasser!
Das hat nicht Rast bei Tag und Nacht,
Ist stets auf Wanderschaft bedacht,
Das Wasser, das Wasser,
Das Wasser, das Wasser.

Das sehn wir auch den Rädern ab,
Den Rädern!
Das sehn wir auch den Rädern ab,
Den Rädern!
Die gar nicht gerne stille stehn,
Die sich mein Tag nicht müde gehn,
Die Räder, die Räder,
Die Räder, die Räder.

1. Wandering

To wander is a miller's joy,
To wander!
To wander is a miller's joy,
To wander!
How useless would a miller be
Who did not wish the world to see?
To wander and wander,
To wander and wander.

We learn it from the water's flow,
The water!
We learn it from the water's flow,
The water!
It never rests by night and day,
It is always rushing on its way,
The water, the water,
The water, the water.

We learn it as the mill wheels turn,
The mill wheels!
We learn it as the mill wheels turn,
The mill wheels!
All day they spin beside the mill,
You never see them standing still,
The mill wheels, the mill wheels,
The mill wheels, the mill wheels.

Die Steine selbst, so schwer sie sind,
Die Steine!
Die Steine selbst, so schwer sie sind,
Die Steine!
Sie tanzen mit den muntern Reihn
Und wollen gar noch schneller sein,
Die Steine, die Steine,
Die Steine, die Steine.

O Wandern, Wandern, meine Lust,
O Wandern!
O Wandern, Wandern, meine Lust,
O Wandern!
Herr Meister und Frau Meisterin,
Lasst mich in Frieden weiter ziehn
Und wandern, und wandern,
Und wandern, und wandern.

The millstone's heavy as they are,
The millstones!
The millstone's heavy as they are,
The millstones!
They join in the merry dance,
Going faster if they have the chance,
The millstones, the millstones,
The millstones, the millstones.

To wander then is my delight,
To wander!
To wander then is my delight,
To wander!
Had I their blessing and goodwill
I'd leave the master and the mill
And wander, and wander,
And wander, and wander.

2. Wohin?

Ich hört' ein Bächlein rauschen
Wohl aus dem Felsenquell,
Hinab zum Tale rauschen
So frisch und wunderhell.

Ich weiss nicht, wie mir wurde,
Nicht, wer den Rat mir gab,
Ich musste auch hinunter
Mit meinem Wanderstab,
Ich musste auch hinunter
Mit meinem Wanderstab.

Hinunter und immer weiter
Und immer dem Bache nach,
Und immer heller rauschte,
Und immer heller der Bach,
Und immer heller rauschte,
Und immer heller der Bach.

Ist das denn meine Strasse?
O Bächlein, sprich, wohin?
Wohin? sprich, wohin?
Du hast mit deinem Rauschen
Mir ganz berauscht den Sinn,
Du hast mit deinem Rauschen
Mir ganz berauscht den Sinn.

2. Whither

I heard a streamlet gushing
From a mountain spring I know,
It's cool fresh water rushing
To the valley down below

I know not what compelled me,
What notion filled my brain,
But I must follow where it goes
With my stout walking cane,
But I must follow where it goes
With my stout walking cane.

So downward ever further
I will follow its rushing flow,
Its even fresher and cooler
The further on I go,
Its even fresher and cooler
The further on I go,

Is this the path to follow?
Oh streamlet tell me where?
Oh where, tell me where?
Did you mean with your babbling
My senses to ensnare?
Did you mean with your babbling
My senses to ensnare?

Was sag' ich denn vom Rauschen? Das kann kein Rauschen sein: Es singen wohl die Nixen Tief unten ihren Reihn, Es singen wohl die Nixen Tief unten ihren Reihn.	Why do I speak of babbling? That sound it cannot be, Is it water nymphs I'm hearing? That dance and sing for me, Is it water nymphs I'm hearing? That dance and sing for me.
Lass singen, Gesell, lass rauschen, Und wandre fröhlich nach! Es gehn ja Mühlenräder In jedem klaren Bach, Es gehn ja Mühlenräder In jedem klaren Bach, Lass singen, Gesell, lass rauschen, Und wandre fröhlich nach, Fröhlich nach, fröhlich nach!	So sing on my friends and babble And go your happy way, In every rushing streamlet the merry mill wheels play, In every rushing streamlet the merry mill wheels play So sing my friends and babble And go your happy way, Happy way, happy way.

3. Halt!

Eine Mühle seh' ich blinken
Aus den Erlen heraus,
Durch Rauschen und Singen
Bricht Rädergebraus,
Bricht Rädergebraus.

Ei willkommen, ei willkommen,
Süsser Mühlengesang!
Ei willkommen, ei willkommen,
Süsser Mühlengesang!
Und das Haus, wie so traulich!
Und die Fenster, wie blank!

Und die Sonne, wie helle
Vom Himmel sie scheint!
Und die Sonne, wie helle
Vom Himmel sie scheint!
Ei, Bächlein, liebes Bächlein,
War es also gemeint?
Ei, Bächlein, liebes Bächlein,
War es also gemeint?
War es also gemeint?
War es also gemeint?

3. Halt by the Brook

See the mill there brightly gleaming,
Through the green elder trees,
The noise of the mill wheels
Joins in the reprise,
Joins in the reprise.

It's so welcome, It's so welcome,
Sweetest song of the mill!
It's so welcome, It's so welcome,
Sweetest song of the mill!
And the house looks so friendly,
And the windows so bright

And the sunlight, its brightness,
From heaven is sent!
The sunlight, its brightness,
From heaven is sent!
Oh streamlet, dearest streamlet,
So was this what you meant?
Oh streamlet, dearest streamlet,
So was this what you meant?
So was this what you meant?
So was this what you meant?

4. Danksagung an den Bach

War es also gemeint,
Mein rauschender Freund,
Dein Singen, dein Klingen,
War es also gemeint
War es also gemeint?

Zur Müllerin hin!
So lautet der Sinn.
Gelt, hab' ich's verstanden,
Hab' ich's verstanden?
Zur Müllerin hin,
Zur Müllerin hin!

Hat sie dich geschickt?
Oder hast mich berückt?
Das möcht' ich noch wissen,
Ob sie dich geschickt,
Ob sie dich geschickt.

Nun wie's auch mag sein,
Ich gebe mich drein:
Was ich such', hab' ich funden,
Wie's immer mag sein.

Nach Arbeit ich frug,
Nun hab' ich genug,
Für die Hände, für's Herze
Vollauf genug,
Vollauf genug!

4. Acknowledgement to the Brook

So was this what you meant,
My fast flowing friend?
Your singing, your babbling,
So was this what you meant?
So was this what you meant?

To the miller's daughter go,
I understand you now, yes,
Is this your message?
Is this your message?
To the fair maiden go,
To the fair maiden go!

Did she send you here?
Or did you charm my ear?
I so want to know,
Was it she sent you here?
Did she send you here?

How ever it may be,
I'll yield willingly,
What I searched for I found it here,
Whatever it may be.

I wanted to work,
I've found all I need
For my hands, and my heart,
All that I need,
All that I need!

5. Am Feierabend

Hätt' ich tausend arme zu rühren!
Könnt' ich brausend die Räder führen!
Könnt' ich wehen durch alle
  Haine!
Könnt' ich drehen alle Steine!
Dass die schöne Müllerin
Merkte meinen treuen Sinn!
Dass die schöne Müllerin
Merkte meinen treuen Sinn!

Ach, wie ist mein Arm so schwach!
Was ich hebe, was ich trage,
Was ich schneide, was ich schlage,
Jeder Knappe tut mir's nach,
Jeder Knappe tut mir's nach.
Und da sitz' ich in der grossen Runde,
In der stillen kühlen Feierstunde,
Und der Meister sagt zu Allen:
"Euer Werk hat mir gefallen,"
"Euer Werk hat mir gefallen."
Und das liebe Mädchen sagt
"Allen eine gute Nacht",
"Allen eine gute Nacht".

Hätt' ich tausend arme zu rühren!
Könnt' ich brausend die Räder führen!
Könnt' ich wehen durch alle
  Haine!
Könnt' ich drehen alle Steine!
Dass die schöne Müllerin
Merkte meinen, meinen treuen Sinn!
Dass die schöne Müllerin
Merkte meinen, meinen treuen Sinn!

Dass die schöne Müllerin
Merkte meinen treuen Sinn!

5. Afterwork

With a thousand arms to aid me,
I could drive all the mill wheels wildly.
With the strength of the storm winds
  blowing,
I could keep the millstones going
So the lovely maiden knew,
That my heart was ever true,
So the lovely maiden knew,
My heart was ever true.

Ah, why are my arms so weak,
What I lift and what I carry
What I chop and what I fell,
Any lad could do as well,
Any lad could do as well.
And I sit where all the family gather,
In the cool of the evening when work is over,
And the Master said with pride,
With your work I'm satisfied,
With your work I'm satisfied.
And the darling maiden said,
"Goodnight all it's time for bed",
"Goodnight all it's time for bed".

With a thousand arms to aid me,
I could drive all the mill wheels wildly.
With the strength of the storm winds
  blowing,
I could keep the millstones going
So the lovely maiden knew,
That my heart, my heart was ever true,
So the lovely maiden knew,
That my heart, my heart was ever true.

So the lovely maiden knew,
That my heart was ever true!

6. Der Neugierige

Ich frage keine Blume,
Ich frage keinen Stern,
Sie können mir alle nicht sagen,
Was ich erführ' so gern.

Ich bin ja auch kein Gärtner,
Die Sterne stehn zu hoch;
Mein Bächlein will ich fragen,
Ob mich mein Herz belog.

O Bächlein meiner Liebe,
Wie bist du heut' so stumm!
Will ja nur Eines wissen,
Ein Wörtchen um und um,
Ein Wörtchen um und um.

Ja, heisst das eine Wörtchen,
Das andre heisset Nein,
Die beiden Wörtchen schliessen
Die ganze Welt mir ein,
Die beiden Wörtchen schliessen
Die ganze Welt mir ein.

O Bächlein meiner Liebe,
Was bist du wunderlich!
Will's ja nicht weiter sagen,
Sag', Bächlein, liebt sie mich?
Sag', Bächlein, liebt sie mich?

6. The Inquirer

I need not ask the flowers,
I'll ask no gleaming star,
Not one of them ever can tell me
What I so long to hear.

Of flowers I know so little,
The stars are far to high,
My little stream will tell me
If my poor heart could lie.

Oh dearest little streamlet,
Today you are serene.
I only want to hear one word,
Over and over again,
One tiny word over again.

Yes, is the word I hope for,
The other word is no,
And these two words embrace
All the world that I know,
And these two words embrace
All the world that I know.

Oh dearest little streamlet,
How wondrous you can be,
My lips are sealed, I give my word,
Say streamlet does she love me?
Say streamlet does she love me?

7. Ungeduld

Ich schnitt' es gern in alle Rinden ein,
Ich grüb' es gern in jeden Kieselstein,
Ich möcht' es sä'n auf jedes frische Beet
Mit Kressensamen, der es schnell verrät,
Auf jeden weissen Zettel möcht' ich's schreiben:
Dein ist mein Herz, dein ist mein Herz,
und soll es ewig, ewig bleiben.

Ich möcht' mir ziehen einen jungen Star,
Bis dass er spräch' die Worte rein und klar,
Bis er sie spräch' mit meines Mundes Klang,
Mit meines Herzens vollem, heissem Drang;
Dann säng' er hell durch ihre Fensterscheiben:
Dein ist mein Herz, dein ist mein Herz,
und soll es ewig, ewig bleiben.

Den Morgenwinden möcht' ich's hauchen ein,
Ich möcht' es säuseln durch den regen Hain;
O, leuchtet' es aus jedem Blumenstern!
Trüg' es der Duft zu ihr von nah und fern!
Ihr Wogen, könnt ihr nichts als Räder treiben?
Dein ist mein Herz, dein ist mein Herz,
und soll es ewig, ewig bleiben.

7. Impatience

I'll carve it on the bark of every tree,
Engrave it into every stone I see,
In flower beds I'll sow the seeds of cress
That quickly grow to show all I express,
On every scrap of paper let me now endorse,
My heart is yours, my heart is yours,
It's yours forever, forever, it's ever yours.

I'd like to train a starling patiently
To say my words so pure and clearly,
To say them with the likeness of my voice,
With all the love that makes my heart rejoice.
Then it could brightly sing before her windowpane
My heart is yours, my heart is yours,
It's yours forever, forever, and ever will remain.

I'll whisper it into the morning breeze,
I'd like to hear it rustling through the trees,
Oh let it shine from every starry flower,
To bring a fragrance to her everywhere.
Oh stream are millwheel songs your only one refrain,
My heart is yours, my heart is yours,
It's yours forever, forever, and ever will remain.

Ich meint', es müsst' in meinen Augen stehen,	I thought it must be shining from my eyes,
Auf meinen Wangen müsst' man's brennen sehn,	And on my burning cheeks where blushes rise,
Zu lesen wär's auf meinem stummen Mund,	Oh on my silent lips it must be read,
Ein jeder Atemzug gäb's laut ihr kund;	And with each breath my thoughts are loudly said
Und sie merkt nichts von all' dem bangen Treiben:	But of my anxious longing she shows no concern
Dein ist mein Herz, dein ist mein Herz, und soll es ewig, ewig bleiben!	My heart is yours, my heart is yours, It's yours forever, forever, and ever will remain.

8. Morgengruss

Guten Morgen, schöne Müllerin!
Wo steckst du gleich das Köpfchen hin,
Als wär' dir was geschehen?
Verdriesst dich denn mein Gruss so
  schwer?
Verstört dich denn mein Blick so sehr?
So muss ich wieder gehen,
So muss ich wieder gehen,
Wieder gehen.

O lass mich nur von ferne stehen,
Nach deinem lieben Fenster sehn,
Von ferne, ganz von ferne!
Du blondes Köpfchen, komm hervor!
Hervor aus eurem runden Tor,
Ihr blauen Morgensterne,
Ihr blauen Morgensterne,
Ihr Morgensterne!

Ihr schlummertrunknen Äugelein,
Ihr taubetrübten
  Blümelein,
Was scheuet ihr die Sonne?
Hat es die Nacht so gut gemeint,
Dass ihr euch schliesst und bückt und
  weint
Nach ihrer stillen Wonne,
Nach ihrer stillen Wonne,
Nach ihrer Wonne?

Nun schüttelt ab der Träume Flor,
Und hebt euch frisch und frei empor
In Gottes hellen Morgen!
Die Lerche wirbelt in der Luft,
Und aus dem tiefen Herzen ruft
Die Liebe Leid und Sorgen,
Die Liebe Leid und Sorgen,
Leid und Sorgen.

8. Morning Greeting

Good morning miller's daughter fair,
Why do you hide away in there?
As if your heart was grieving.
Could you not even say
  hello?
or does my glance displease you so?
Then I will now be leaving,
Then I will now be leaving,
I will be leaving.

Oh let me only stand again,
And gaze at your dear windowpane,
But only from afar.
Oh little golden head appear,
Come forth those round blue eyes so clear,
And shine like morning stars,
And shine like morning stars,
Like morning stars.

Oh eyes still closed where dreams pursue,
Oh dainty flowers weighed down with
  dew,
Why do you hide from sunlight?
Was it a pleasant night of sleep?
Made you bow down and close and
  weep,
For all her silent delight,
For all her silent delight,
Her silent delight.

Your veil of dreams can now be shed,
And bright and freely raise your head
To greet God's radiant day break.
The lark trills higher in the skies,
Yet deep within my heart there cries
The pain of love and heartache,
The pain of love and heartache,
Love and heartache.

9. Des Müllers Blumen

Am Bach viel kleine Blumen stehen,
Aus hellen blauen Augen sehn;
Der Bach der ist des Müllers
   Freund,
Und hellblau Liebchens
   Auge scheint;
Drum sind es meine Blumen,
Drum sind es meine Blumen.

Dicht unter ihrem Fensterlein
Da will ich pflanzen die Blumen ein,
Da ruft ihr zu, wenn alles schweigt,
Wenn sich ihr Haupt zum Schlummer
   neigt,
Ihr wisst ja, was ich meine,
Ihr wisst ja, was ich meine.

Und wenn sie tät die Äuglein zu,
Und schläft in süsser, süsser Ruh',
Dann lispelt als ein Traumgesicht Ihr
   zu:
"Vergiss, vergiss mein nicht!"
Das ist es, was ich meine,
Das ist es, was ich meine.

Und schliesst sie früh die Laden auf,
Dann schaut mit Liebesblick hinauf:
Der Tau in euren Äugelein,
Das sollen meine Tränen sein,
Die will ich auf euch weinen,
Die will ich auf euch weinen.

9. The Miller's Flowers

Along the stream grow little blue flowers,
They gaze up at me like clear blue eyes;
The stream and the miller in friendship
   unite,
My sweetheart's blue eyes are shining
   bright;
So they are my own flowers,
So they are my own flowers.

I'll kneel beneath her windowsill
And plant my flowers when all is still,
And when at night she lays her head,
They'll call to her the words
   I've said,
Yes, they know all my heart's desires,
Yes, they know all my heart's desires.

And when her eyes in slumber close,
She'll sleep in sweetest, sweet repose,
And while she dreams still
   whisper yet;
"Forget me not, do not forget".
That is what I would want to say,
That is what I would want to say.

She opens her shutters at break of day,
Then gaze towards her lovingly;
And in your eyes the morning dew,
Are all the tears I wept on you,
From all my silent weeping,
From all my silent weeping.

10. Tränenregen

Wir sassen so traulich beisammen
Im kühlen Erlendach,
Wir schauten so traulich zusammen
Hinab in den rieselnden Bach.
Der Mond war auch gekommen,
Die Sternlein hinterdrein,
Und schauten so traulich zusammen
In den silbernen Spiegel hinein.

Ich sah nach keinem Monde,
Nach keinem Sternenschein,
Ich schaute nach ihrem Bilde,
Nach ihren Augen allein.
Und sahe sie nicken und blicken
Herauf aus dem seligen Bach,
Die Blümlein am Ufer, die blauen,
Sie nickten und blickten ihr nach.

10. Teardrops

We sat so closely together
Where elder trees gave shade,
So happy to be with each other
We watched where the waters cascade.
The moon appeared above us,
The stars began to gleam,
They closely watched us together
In the mirror of the stream.

The moon was no distraction,
Nor were the stars that shine,
I only saw her reflection,
And only her eyes held mine.
I watched the nodding and dancing
Up from the happy brook,
The little blue flowers around us,
Reflected her nod and her look.

Und in den Bach versunken
Der ganze Himmel schien,
Und wollte mich mit hinunter
In seine Tiefe ziehn.
Und über den Wolken und Sternen
Da rieselte munter der Bach,
Und rief mit Singen und Klingen:
"Geselle, Geselle, mir nach!"

Da gingen die Augen mir
    über,
Da ward es im Spiegel so kraus;
Sie sprach: "Es kommt ein Regen,
Ade! ich geh' nach Haus."

And then below the water
The whole bright sky appeared,
It wanted to lure me downward
Into its deepest bed.
And over the clouds and the stars below
The merry stream rippled along,
And called to me, brother, my brother
Come and follow my murmuring song.

And then our smooth mirror was
    ruffled,
From tears that I could not restrain,
She said I must go home now,
"Goodbye, it's starting to rain."

11. Mein!

Bächlein, lass dein Rauschen sein!
Räder, stellt eur Brausen ein!
All' ihr muntern Waldvögeln,
Gross und klein,
Endet eure Melodein,
Endet eure Melodein!

Durch den Hain
Aus und ein
Schalle heut' ein Reim allein,
Durch den Hain
Aus und ein
Schalle heut' ein Reim allein:
Die geliebte Müllerin ist mein, ist mein,
Die geliebte Müllerin ist mein, ist mein,
Mein, Mein!

Frühling, sind das alle deine
    Blümelein?
Sonne, hast du keinen hellern Schein?
Ach, so muss ich ganz allein,
Mit dem seligen Worte mein,
Unverstanden in der weiten
    Schöpfung sein,
Unverstanden in der weiten
    Schöpfung sein.

11. Mine

Streamlet rush along no more!
Millwheels cease your endless roar!
And you merry songbirds all,
Large and small,
End your melodious call,
End your melodious call.

Through the trees,
On the breeze,
Let this day hear one reprise.
Through the trees,
On the breeze,
Let this day hear one reprise,
That the miller's daughter is mine, is mine,
That the miller's daughter is mine, is mine,
Mine, mine!

Springtime, are these little flowers your
    best display?
Sun, have you no more brighter ray?
Ah, I must be quite alone
With that precious word, my own,
Understood by no one in
    creation,
Understood by no one in
    creation.

Bächlein, lass dein Rauschen sein!	Streamlet rush along no more!
Räder, stellt eur Brausen ein!	Millwheels cease your endless roar!
All' ihr muntern Waldvögeln,	And you merry songbirds all,
Gross und klein,	Large and small,
Endet eure Melodein,	End your melodious call,
Endet eure Melodein!	End your melodious call!
Durch den Hain	Through the trees,
Aus und ein	On the breeze,
Schalle heut' ein Reim allein,	Let this day hear one reprise.
Durch den Hain	Through the trees,
Aus und ein	On the breeze,
Schalle heut' ein Reim allein:	Let this day hear one reprise,
Die geliebte Müllerin ist mein, ist mein,	That the miller's daughter is mine, is mine,
Die geliebte Müllerin ist mein, ist mein,	That the miller's daughter is mine, is mine,
Mein, Mein!	Mine, is mine!

12. Pause

Meine Laute hab' ich gehängt an die Wand,
Hab' sie umschlungen mit einem grünen Band
Ich kann nicht mehr singen, mein Herz ist zu voll,
Weiss nicht, wie ich's in Reime zwingen soll.
Meiner Sehnsucht allerheissesten Schmerz
Durft' ich aushauchen in Liederscherz,
Und wie ich klagte so süss und fein,
Glaubt' ich doch, mein Leiden wär' nicht klein.
Ei, wie gross ist wohl meines Glückes Last,
Dass kein Klang auf Erden es in sich fasst,
Dass kein Klang auf Erden es in sich fasst?

Nun, liebe Laute, ruh' an dem Nagel hier!
Und weht ein Lüftchen über die Saiten dir,
Und streift eine Biene mit ihren Flügeln dich,
Da wird mir so bange und es durchschauert mich.
Warum liess ich das Band auch hängen so lang'?
Oft fliegt's um die Saiten mit seufzendem Klang.
Ist es der Nachklang meiner Liebespein?
Soll es das Vorspiel neuer Lieder sein?
Ist es der Nachklang meiner Liebespein?
Soll es das Vorspiel neuer Lieder sein?

12. Pause

Now my lute is to the wall consigned,
And a green ribbon I have around it entwined.
My heart is so full, what songs can there be?
No more can its sweet rhymes be drawn from me.
All my longing, all the burning pain
Could be eased in a lighthearted song once again,
And my lamenting so gentle and sweet,
Knowing that my suffering was so great,
Oh how heavy this joy weighs on my heart,
That no sound on all the earth can from it part,
That no sound on earth can from it part.

So dearest lute now rest there on your nail,
And when the breezes sighing pass over your strings,
Or bees passing by may brush you with their wings,
Then I'll be uneasy, fear will then prevail.
Oh why, why did I leave the ribbon hanging long?
Fluttering on the strings often breathing a song.
Is it the echo of my loves pain?
Is it a prelude to new songs again?
Is it the echo of my loves pain?
Is it a prelude to new songs again?

13. Mit dem grünen Lautenbande

Schad' um das schöne grüne Band,
Dass es verbleicht hier an der Wand,
Ich hab' das Grün so gern,
Ich hab' das Grün so gern!
So sprachst du, Liebchen, heut' zu mir;
Gleich knüpf' ich's ab und send' es dir:
Nun hab' das Grüne gern,
Nun hab' das Grüne gern!

Ist auch dein ganzer Liebster weiss,
Soll Grün doch haben seinen Preis,
Und ich auch hab' es gern,
Und ich auch hab' es gern.
Weil unsre Lieb' ist immergrün,
Weil grün der Hoffnung Fernen blühn,
Drum haben wir es gern,
Drum haben wir es gern.

Nun schlinge in die Locken dein
Das grüne Band gefällig ein,
Du hast ja's Grün so gern,
Du hast ja's Grün so gern.
Dann weiss ich, wo die Hoffnung
  wohnt,
Dann weiss ich, wo die
  Liebe thront,
Dann hab' ich's Grün erst gern,
Dann hab' ich's Grün erst gern.

13. The Green Ribbon

That lovely ribbon green as jade,
It's sad to leave it there to fade,
And I'm so fond of green,
And I'm so fond of green!
That's what my sweetheart said today,
I'll send it to her right away,
For she is fond of green,
For she is fond of green.

Though he you love is pale and white,
It's green that gives you most delight,
So I am also fond of green,
I'm also fond of green.
Since distance proves that hope is green,
So evergreen will love remain,
That's why we are so fond of green,
That's why we are so fond of green.

Now take the ribbon and with care
Entwine it fondly in your hair,
You are so fond of green,
You are so fond of green.
Then I know where my hope
  is found,
Then I'll know where my love's
  enthroned,
Then I shall really love green,
Then I shall really love green.

14. Der Jäger

Was sucht denn der Jäger am Mühlbach hier?
Bleib', trotziger Jäger, in deinem Revier!
Hier gibt es kein Wild zu jagen für dich,
Hier wohnt nur ein Rehlein, ein zahmes, für mich.
Und willst du das zärtliche Rehlein sehn,
So lass deine Büchsen im Walde stehn,
Und lass deine klaffenden Hunde zu Haus,
Und lass auf dem Horne den Saus und Braus,
Und scheere vom Kinne das struppige Haar,
Sonst scheut sich im Garten das Rehlein fürwahr,
Und scheere vom Kinne das struppige Haar,
Sonst scheut sich im Garten das Rehlein fürwahr.

14. The Hunter

Now what does the hunter seek here by the mill?
For here there's no hunting, no game can he kill!
So impudent hunter stay in your domain,
there's just a tame doe here and mine she'll remain.
And if my young doe you are wanting to meet,
Your rifle must stay in the woods out of sight,
And leave all your yelping hound dogs at home,
And stop all that noise with your hunting horn,
And shave from your chin all that bristly hair,
Unless my young doe you are wanting to scare,
And shave from your chin all that bristly hair,
Unless my young doe you are wanting to scare.

Doch besser, du bliebest im Walde dazu,	Still better stay deep in the woods where you're known,
Und liessest die Mühlen und Müller in Ruh'.	And go from the mill and leave millers alone,
Was taugen die Fischlein im grünen Gezweig?	What would fishes do in the branch of a tree?
Was will denn das Eichhorn im bläulichen Teich?	And what would a squirrel do in the blue sea?
Drum bleibe, du trotziger Jäger, im Hain,	So impudent huntsman stay where you belong,
Und lass mich mit meinen drei Rädern allein;	The millwheels are mine and they turn to my song;
Und willst meinem Schätzchen dich machen beliebt	But if its my sweetheart you want in the end,
So wisse, mein Freund, was ihr Herzchen betrüht:	Then, know you what troubles her heart my friend,
Die Eber, die kommen zur Nacht aus dem Hain,	It's during the night when wild boars root around,
Und brechen in ihren Kohlgarten ein,	And trample her cabbage patch into the ground,
Und treten und wühlen herum in dem Feld:	So if it's a hero you want her to see,
Die Eber die schiesse, du Jägerheld!	Then shoot the wild boars and a hero you'll be!

15. Eifersucht und Stolz

Wohin so schnell, so kraus und wild,
  mein lieber Bach?
Eilst du voll Zorn dem frechen Bruder
  Jäger nach?
Kehr' um, kehr' um, und schilt erst deine
  Müllerin
Für ihren leichten, losen, kleinen
  Flattersinn.
Kehr' um, kehr' um, kehr' um.

Sahst du sie gestern abend nicht am
  Tore stehn,
Mit langem Halse nach der grossen
  Strasse sehn?
Wenn von dem Fang der Jäger lustig
  zieht nach Haus,
Da steckt kein sittsam Kind den Kopf
  zum Fenster 'naus.
Wenn von dem Fang der Jäger lustig
  zieht nach Haus,
Da steckt kein sittsam Kind den Kopf
  zum Fenster 'naus.
Geh', Bächlein, hin und sag' ihr das,
Geh', Bächlein, hin und sag' ihr das,
  doch sag' ihr nicht,
Hörst du, kein Wort, von meinem
  traurigen Gesicht;

15. Jealousy and Pride

Beloved stream why flow so fast and
  wild today?
Do you enraged pursue the huntsman
  on his way?
Turn back, turn back and scold the
  miller's daughter first,
For all the fickleness her wanton ways
  suggest,
Turn back, turn back, turn back.

Did you not see her last night standing
  at the gate?
Her long neck craning looking down the
  road so late,
When from the hunt the huntsman
  carries home the kill,
What modest girl would lean across her
  window sill?
When from the hunt the huntsman
  carries home the kill,
What modest girl would lean across her
  window sill?
Go streamlet, go say that to her,
Go streamlet and say that to her,
But not one word,
hear me, no word, about my melancholy
  face.

Sag' ihr: Er schnitzt bei mir sich eine Pfeif' aus Rohr, Und bläst den Kindern schöne Tänz' und Lieder vor. Sag' ihr, Sag' ihr: Er schnitzt bei mir sich eine Pfeif' aus Rohr, Sag' ihr, Sag' ihr: Er bläst den Kindern schöne Tänz' und Lieder vor, Sag ihr's, sag ihr's, sag ihr's!	Say this he cuts a reed to make a pipe to play, And blows for children pretty songs and dances gay, Say this, say this, He cuts a reed to make a pipe to play, Say this, say this, He blows for children pretty songs and dances gay, Say this, say this, say this!

16. Die liebe Farbe

In Grün will ich mich kleiden,
In grüne Tränenweiden,
Mein Schatz hat's Grün so gern,
Mein Schatz hat's Grün so gern.
Will suchen einen Zypressenhain,
Eine Heide von grünem Rosmarein,
Mein Schatz hat's Grün so gern,
Mein Schatz hat's Grün so gern.

Wohlauf zum fröhlichen Jagen!
Wohlauf durch Heid' und Hagen!
Mein Schatz hat's Jagen so gern,
Mein Schatz hat's Jagen so gern.
Das Wild, das ich jage, das ist der Tod,
Die Heide, die heiss ich die Liebesnot,
Mein Schatz hat's Jagen so gern,
Mein Schatz hat's Jagen so gern.

Grabt mir ein Grab im Wasen,
Deckt mich mit grünem Rasen,
Mein Schatz hat's Grün so gern,
Mein Schatz hat's Grün so gern.
Kein Kreuzlein schwarz, kein Blümlein bunt,
Grün, alles grün so rings und rund!
Mein Schatz hat's Grün so gern,
Mein Schatz hat's Grün so gern.

16. The Favourite Colour

I'll dress in green for sorrow,
The green of weeping willow,
My love is fond of green,
My love is fond of green.
I'll find a cypress sanctuary,
Or a heath of the greenest rosemary,
My love is fond of green,
My love is fond of green.

Away thro heathland and meadow,
The merry hunt to follow,
My love is fond of the hunt,
My love is fond of the hunt.
The game I will seek is that of death,
The heathland, I'll call it my path of grief,
My love is fond of the hunt,
My love is fond of the hunt.

Dig me a grave in clover,
With greenest turf to cover,
My love is fond of green,
My love is fond of green.
No cross of black, no flowers that fade,
Green, only green where I am laid,
My love is fond of green,
My love is fond of green.

17. Die böse Farbe

Ich möchte ziehn in die Welt hinaus,
Hinaus in die weite Welt,
Wenn's nur so grün, so grün nicht wär'
Da draussen in Wald und Feld!

Ich möchte die grünen Blätter all'
Pflücken von jedem Zweig,
Ich möchte die grünen Gräser all'
Weinen ganz totenbleich,
Weinen ganz totenbleich.

Ach Grün, du böse Farbe du,
Was siehst mich immer an,
So stolz, so keck, so schadenfroh,
Mich armen, armen weissen Mann?

Ich möchte liegen vor ihrer Tür,
Im Sturm und Regen und Schnee,
Und singen ganz leise bei Tag und Nacht
Das eine Wörtchen Ade,
Das eine Wörtchen Ade!

Horch, wenn im Wald ein Jagdhorn
 schallt,
Da klingt ihr Fensterlein,
Und schaut sie auch nach mir nicht aus,
Darf ich doch schauen hinein.

O binde von der Stirn dir ab
Das grüne, grüne Band,
Das grüne, grüne Band.
Ade, Ade! und reiche mir
Zum Abschied deine Hand!
Ade, Ade! und reiche mir
Zum Abschied deine Hand,
Zum Abschied deine Hand!

17. The Odious Colour

I'd like to leave and in the world go forth,
Go forth now to see the wide world,
If it were not so green
Out there in forest and in the field.

I'd like to strip all the leaves so green
From every branch in sight,
I'd like then to weep on the grass so green,
Weep, till it's deathly white,
Weep, till it's deathly white.

Ah green, I hate the colour now,
It looks at me always,
So proud, so brash, so gloatingly,
And me a pale and wretched man.

I'd like to lie down before her door,
in storm, in rain and hail,
And softly I'd sing by day and night,
The word I'd sing is farewell,
The word I would sing is farewell.

Yet when the hunting horn shall
 sound,
Then clicks her window latch,
And though she does not look for me,
A sight of her I may catch.

Untie that ribbon from your brow,
That green, green band,
That green, green band.
Farewell, farewell but give to me
Once more a parting hand,
Farewell, farewell but give to me
Once more a parting hand,
Once more a parting hand.

18. Trockne Blumen

Ihr Blümlein alle,
Die sie mir gab,
Euch soll man legen
Mit mir ins Grab.

Wie seht ihr alle
Mich an so weh,
Als ob ihr wüsstet,
Wie mir gescheh'?

Ihr Blümlein alle,
Wie welk, wie blass?
Ihr Blümlein alle
Wovon so nass?

Ach, Tränen machen
Nicht maiengrün,
Machen tote Liebe
Nicht wieder blühn.

Und Lenz wird kommen
Und Winter wird gehen,
Und Blümlein werden
Im Grase stehn.

Und Blümlein liegen
In meinem Grab,
Die Blümlein alle,
Die sie mir gab.

18. Withered Flowers

You little flowers
That to me she gave,
Shall all lie with me
In my cool grave.

You gaze at me
With such sympathy,
Do you then know
What is happening to me?

You little flowers
So sad, so pale,
Why are you all
So moist, so frail?

Ah, tears will not make
The green spring return,
And a love that's dead
Cannot blossom again.

Yet spring will come,
And the winter will pass,
And flowers will bloom
Once more in the grass.

The little flowers
Lying in my grave,
Are all the flowers
That to me she gave.

Und wenn sie wandelt	And when she wanders
Am Hügel vorbei,	By the mound where I'm laid,
Und denkt im Herzen:	Her heart will say,
"Der meint' es treu!"	"For true love he died"
Dann Blümlein alle,	Then all you flowers
Heraus, heraus!	Come out at last,
Der Mai ist kommen,	For spring is here
Der Winter ist aus.	And the winter has past.
Und wenn sie wandelt	And when she wanders
Am Hügel vorbei,	By the mound where I'm laid,
Und denkt im Herzen:	Her heart will say,
"Der meint' es treu!"	"For true love he died"
Dann Blümlein alle,	Then all you flowers
Heraus, heraus!	Come out at last,
Der Mai ist kommen,	For spring is here
Der Winter ist aus.	And the winter has past.
Dann Blümlein alle,	Then all you flowers
Heraus, heraus!	Come out at last,
Der Mai ist kommen,	For spring is here
Der Winter ist aus.	And the winter has past.

19. Der Müller und der Bach

DER MÜLLER:
Wo ein treues Herze
In Liebe vergeht,
Da welken die Lilien
Auf jedem Beet.

Da muss in die Wolken
Der Vollmond gehen,
Damit seine Tränen
Die Menschen nicht sehn.

Da halten die Englein
Die Augen sich zu,
Und schluchzen und singen
Die Seele zu Ruh'.

DER BACH:
Und wenn sich die Liebe
Dem Schmerz entringt,
Ein Sternlein, ein neues
Am Himmel erblinkt,
Ein Sternlein, ein neues
Am Himmel erblinkt.

Da springen drei Rosen,
Halb rot und halb weiss,
Die welken nicht wieder
Aus Dornenreis.

Und die Engelein schneiden
Die Flügel sich ab,
Und gehn alle Morgen
Zur Erde herab,
Und gehn alle Morgen
Zur Erde herab.

19. The Miller and the Brook

THE MILLER:
When a heart so faithful
from love has died,
In every flower bed
the lilies fade.

And into the veiling clouds
the full moon must flee,
Concealing her tear drops
so no man may see.

And dear little angels
will cover up their eyes,
And sobbing will calm the soul
with sweet lullabies.

THE BROOK:
And when love is striving
from sorrow to fly,
A new star that brightly shines
appears in the sky,
A new star that brightly shines
appears in the sky.

Then three roses open,
half white and half red,
Which never will whither
on their thorny bed.

And the dear little angels
are clipping their wings,
And come down upon the earth
to see what each morning brings,
And come down upon the earth
to see what each morning brings.

DER MÜLLER:
Ach, Bächlein, liebes Bächlein,
Du meinst es so gut:
Ach, Bächlein, aber weisst du,
Wie Liebe tut?

Ach, unten, da unten,
Die kühle Ruh'!
Ach, Bächlein, liebes Bächlein,
So singe nur zu,
Ach, Bächlein, liebes Bächlein,
So singe nur zu.

THE MILLER:
Oh streamlet, dearest streamlet,
So kind and so true,
But streamlet do you really know
What love can do?

Ah under your surface lies
A cooling peace,
Ah, streamlet, dearest streamlet,
sing on and never cease,
Ah, streamlet, dearest streamlet,
sing on and never cease.

20. Des Baches Wiegenlied

Gute Ruh', gute Ruh'!
Tu' die Augen zu!
Gute Ruh', gute Ruh'!
Tu' die Augen zu!
Wandrer, du müder, du bist zu Haus.
Die Treu' ist hier,
Sollst liegen bei mir,
Die Treu' ist hier,
Sollst liegen bei mir,
Bis das Meer will trinken die Bächlein aus,
Bis das Meer will trinken die Bächlein aus.

Will betten dich kühl,
Auf weichen Pfühl,
Will betten dich kühl,
Auf weichen Pfühl.
In dem blauen krystallenen Kämmerlein.
Heran, heran,
Was wiegen kann,
Heran, heran,
Was wiegen kann,
Woget und wieget den Knaben mir ein,
Woget und wieget den Knaben mir ein!

20. The Brook's Lullaby

Close your eyes, close your eyes
to my lullabies,
Close your eyes, close your eyes
to my lullabies,
Weary wanderer you are home at last.
Rest here with me
and find constancy,
Rest here with me
and find constancy.
Till the stream is embraced by the ocean so vast,
Till the stream is embraced by the ocean so vast.

On a pillow I've made,
let your head be laid,
On a pillow I've made,
let your head be laid,
In a small chamber where crystal blue waters lie.
Ever on, ever on,
and cradle my son,
Ever on, ever on
and cradle my son.
Rock him to sleep with a sweet lullaby,
Rock him to sleep with a sweet lullaby.

Wenn ein Jagdhorn schallt
Aus dem grünen Wald,
Wenn ein Jagdhorn schallt
Aus dem grünen Wald,
Will ich sausen und brausen wohl um
  dich her.
Blickt nicht herein,
Blaue Blümelein,
Blickt nicht herein,
Blaue Blümelein!
Ihr macht meinem Schläfer die Träume
  so schwer,
Ihr macht meinem Schläfer die Träume
  so schwer.

Hinweg, hinweg
Von dem Mühlensteg,
Hinweg, hinweg
Böses Mägdelein,
dass ihn dein Schatten, dein Schatten
  nicht weckt!
Wirf mir herein
Dein Tüchlein fein,
Wirf mir herein
Dein Tüchlein fein,
Dass ich die Augen ihm halte bedeckt,
Dass ich die Augen ihm halte bedeckt!

Gute Nacht, gute Nacht!
Bis alles wacht,
Gute Nacht, gute Nacht!
Bis alles wacht,
Schlaf' aus deine Freude, schlaf' aus
  dein Leid!

When the horn and the hound
Through the green wood sound,
When the horn and the hound
Through the green wood sound,
In a surging torrent I'll stir up the
  streams.
Let him sleep,
flowers of blue, do not peep,
Let him sleep,
flowers of blue, do not peep.
You may cause my sleeper to grieve in
  his dreams,
You may cause my sleeper to grieve in
  his dreams.

Go away wretched girl,
from the mill path stay,
Go away wretched girl,
from the mill path stay,
Lest your shadow may cause him to
  wake.
And as you leave
throw in your handkerchief,
And as you leave
throw in your handkerchief.
And for his eyes a fine cover I'll make,
And for his eyes a fine cover I'll make.

Goodnight, goodnight,
till all is light,
Goodnight, goodnight,
till all is light.
Sleep thru your happiness, and sleep
  thru your pain.

Der Vollmond steigt,	The full moon appears,
Der Nebel weicht,	the mist soon clears,
Der Vollmond steigt,	The full moon appears,
Der Nebel weicht,	the mist soon clears,
Und der Himmel da droben, wie ist er so weit,	And the heaven above us so vast will remain,
Und der Himmel da droben, wie ist er so weit!	And the heaven above us so vast will remain.

Franz Schubert

Winterreise – The Winter Journey

Die Winterreise was composed in 1827; fourteen of the songs in the Spring, the rest in the Autumn. The poems, written by Wilhelm Muller, concern a young man, disappointed in love, wandering through the bleak winter landscape.

"Schubert had been ill for a long time and had known some unhappy experiences. The rosy gleam had disappeared from his life and winter had come to him in earnest. The poet's despairing tone attracted him" (Johann Mayrhofer's 'Recollections').

Schubert's friend, Joseph Von Spaun, related:

"To my query, what was the matter with him, he only answered, "You will soon understand". One day he said to me "Come to Schober's this evening. I shall sing a garland of lugubrious songs for you. I very much want to know what you all think of them. They have had a greater effect on me than any other songs". He sang the whole of Die Winterreise in a voice filled with emotion. We were astonished by the sombre mood of the songs and, at the end Schober said that there was only one song he liked – Der Lindenbaum. Schubert said, "I like these songs better than all my others and you will also come to like them". He was right, for we were soon enthusiastic about these sad songs, so beautifully sung by Vogl".

Schubert was paid one gilden for the song. The correction of the proofs was the last work he did before his death.

1. Gute Nacht

Fremd bin ich eingezogen,
Fremd zieh' ich wieder aus.
Der Mai war mir gewogen
Mit manchem Blumenstrauß.
Das Mädchen sprach von Liebe,
Die Mutter gar von Eh',
Das Mädchen sprach von Liebe,
Die Mutter gar von Eh',
Nun ist die Welt so trübe,
Der Weg gehüllt in Schnee.
Nun ist die Welt so trübe,
Der Weg gehüllt in Schnee

Ich kann zu meiner Reisen
Nicht wählen mit der Zeit,
Muß selbst den Weg mir weisen
In dieser Dunkelheit.
Es zieht ein Mondenschatten
Als mein Gefährte mit,
Es zieht ein Mondenschatten
Als mein Gefährte mit,
Und auf den weißen Matten
Such' ich des Wildes Tritt.
Und auf den weißen Matten
Such' ich des Wildes Tritt.

Was soll ich länger weilen,
Daß man mich trieb hinaus?
Laß irre Hunde heulen
Vor ihres Herren Haus;
Die Liebe liebt das Wandern
Gott hat sie so gemacht –
Von einem zu dem andern.
Gott hat sie so gemacht
Die Liebe liebt das Wandern
Fein Liebchen, gute Nacht!
Von einem zu dem andern.
Fein Liebchen, gute Nacht!

1. Goodnight

I came here as a stranger,
A stranger I depart.
I came when May was blossoming
And Joy was in my heart.
I met a girl who spoke of love,
Our wedding day was planned.
Her mother gave her blessing,
I soon would take her hand.
But now the sky is overcast,
Deep snow lies on the land,
But now the sky is overcast,
Deep snow lies on the land.

I cannot choose the time to leave,
My journey must be now,
And though I walk in darkness,
I'll find my way somehow.
The moon has cast my shadow,
    Together we will go,
The tracks of deer will guide my way
Across the fields of snow.
The moon has cast my shadow,
    Together we will go,
The tracks of deer will guide my way
Across the fields of snow.

Why need I stay here longer?
Why should I bear their spite?
What care I for their howling dogs
That guard their gates at night?
Love wanders where it pleases,
God made it in his sight,
It breaks the heart it seizes,
And so my love, goodnight.
Love wanders where it pleases,
God made it in his sight,
It breaks the heart it seizes,
And so my love, goodnight.

Will dich im Traum nicht stören,	I'll not disturb your dreaming,
Wär schad' um deine Ruh',	Why spoil a sleep so pure,
Sollst meinen Tritt nicht hören	You will not hear my leaving,
Sacht, sacht die Türe zu!	I'll softly close the door.
Schreibe im Vorubergehen	And on your gate I'll write 'Goodnight',
Ans Tor dir, gute Nacht,	As I am passing through,
Damit du mögest sehen,	So when you chance to see it
An dich hab' ich gedacht.	You'll know I thought of you.
Schreibe im Vorubergehen	I'll write 'Goodnight' upon your gate
Ans Tor dir, gute Nacht,	As I am passing through,
Damit du mögest sehen,	And when you chance to see it
An dich hab' ich gedacht,	You'll know I thought of you,
An dich hab' ich gedacht.	You'll know I thought of you.

2. Die Wetterfahne

Der Wind spielt mit der
   Wetterfahne
auf meines schönen Liebchens Haus.
Da dacht ich schon in meinem Wahne,
sie pfiff den armen Flüchtling aus.

Er hätt' es ehr bemerken sollen,
des Hauses aufgestecktes Schild,
so hätt' er nimmer suchen wollen
im Haus ein treues
   Frauenbild.

Der Wind spielt drinnen mit den
   Herzen
wie auf dem Dach, nur nicht so laut.
Was fragen sie nach meinen Schmerzen?
Ihr Kind ist eine reiche Braut.

Der Wind spielt drinnen mit den
   Herzen
wie auf dem Dach, nur nicht so laut.
Was fragen sie nach meinen Schmerzen?
Was fragen sie nach meinen Schmerzen?
Ihr Kind ist eine reiche Braut.

2. The Weathervane

The wind is playing with the
   weathervane
Over the house where my sweetheart lives,
And so it seems in my confusion
It hisses and mocks this fugitive.

If I had noticed the warning sooner,
And heeded the sign of the weathervane,
Then I would never have sought the love
Of the faithless woman who caused this
   pain.

The wind is playing with hearts inside
   the house,
As on the roof, but not so loud.
What do they care about my grieving?
Their daughter is a wealthy bride.

The wind is playing with hearts inside
   the house,
As on the roof, but not so loud.
What do they care about my grieving?
What do they care about my grieving?
Their daughter is a wealthy bride.

3. Gefror'ne Tränen

Gefror'ne Tränen fallen
von meinen Wangen ab:
Ob es mir denn entgangen,
daß ich geweinet hab'?
daß ich geweinet hab'?

Ei Tränen, meine Tränen,
und seid ihr gar so lau,
daß ihr erstarrt zu Eise
wie kühler Morgentau?

Und dringt doch aus der Quelle
der Brust so glühend heiß,
als wolltet ihr zerschmelzen
des ganzen Winters Eis!
des ganzen Winters Eis!
Und dringt doch aus der Quelle
der Brust so glühend heiß,
als wolltet ihr zerschmelzen
des ganzen Winters Eis!
des ganzen Winters Eis!

3. Frozen Teardrops

I feel the teardrops freezing
As they fall from my eyes,
How long I had been weeping
I did not realise,
I did not realise.

Oh teardrops, my own teardrops,
How can you be so cool?
How could you freeze so quickly
Like early morning dew?

And yet you spring within me,
So burning hot you rise,
As if to melt the winter
With all its snow and ice,
With all its snow and ice.
And yet you spring within me,
So burning hot you rise,
As if to melt the winter,
With all its snow and ice,
With all its snow and ice.

4. Erstarrung

Ich such' im Schnee vergebens
nach ihrer Tritte Spur,
wo sie an meinem Arme
durchstrich die grüne Flur.

Ich such' im Schnee vergebens
nach ihrer Tritte Spur,
wo sie an meinem Arme
durchstrich die grüne Flur.

Ich will den Boden küssen,
durchdringen Eis und Schnee
mit meinen heißen Tränen,
bis ich die Erde, die Erde seh'

Ich will den Boden küssen,
durchdringen Eis und Schnee
mit meinen heißen Tränen,
bis ich die Erde, die Erde seh'

Wo find' ich eine Blüte,
wo find' ich grünes Gras?
Die Blumen sind erstorben
der Rasen sieht so blaß.

Die Blumen sind erstorben
der Rasen sieht so blaß.
Wo find' ich eine Blüte,
wo find' ich grünes Gras?

Soll denn kein Angedenken
ich nehmen mit von hier?
Wenn meine Schmerzen schweigen,
wer sagt mir dann von ihr?

Soll denn kein Angedenken
ich nehmen mit von hier?
Wenn meine Schmerzen schweigen,
wer sagt mir dann von ihr?

4. Numbness

I search the snow so vainly,
No footprints can be seen,
Where hand in hand we wandered
In meadows flesh and green.

I'm searching for her footprints,
But no trace can I find,
Where arm in arm we roamed the fields
When love was fresh and blind.

I'll kiss the frozen meadows,
To pierce the ice and snow
With all my burning teardrops,
And see the earth, the earth below.

I long to kiss the meadows,
And melt the ice and snow
With all my burning teardrops,
To see the earth, the earth below.

Where can I find a flower?
Where are the fields of green?
The flowers all have died away,
No blade of grass is seen.

The flowers all have died away,
No blade of grass is seen.
Where can I find a flower?
Where are the fields of green?

Can I then find no keepsake
That I can take from here?
When all my sorrows leave me,
Who will speak to me of her?

I need to find a keepsake
To take away from here,
When all my pain is ended
Who then will speak of her?

Mein Herz ist wie erfroren,
kalt starrt ihr Bild darin:
Schmilzt je das Herz mir wieder
fließt auch ihr Bild, ihr Bild dahin

Mein Herz ist wie erfroren,
kalt starrt ihr Bild darin:
Schmilzt je das Herz mir wieder
fließt auch ihr Bild, ihr Bild dahin,
ihr Bild dahin.

My heart to ice is frozen,
And cold there she is laid,
So thaw my heart, Oh thaw again
And then her image will quickly fade.

My heart to ice has frozen,
And cold there she is laid,
So thaw my heart, Oh thaw again,
And then her image will quickly fade,
Will quickly fade.

5. Der Lindenbaum

Brunnen vor dem Tore,
da steht ein Lindenbaum:
Ich träumt in seinem Schatten
so manchen süßen Traum.

Ich schnitt in seine Rinde
so manches liebe Wort;
es zog in Freud' und Leide
zu ihm mich immer fort.

Ich mußt' auch heute wandern
vorbei in tiefer Nacht,
da hab' ich noch im Dunkel
die Augen zugemacht.

Und seine Zweige rauschten,
als riefen sie mir zu:
Komm her zu mir, Geselle,
hier find'st du deine Ruh'!

Die kalten Winde bliesen
mir grad ins Angesicht;
der Hut flog mir vom Kopfe,
ich wendete mich nicht.

Nun bin ich manche Stunde
entfernt von jenem Ort,
und immer hör' ich's rauschen:
Du fändest Ruhe dort!

Nun bin ich manche Stunde
entfernt von jenem Ort,
und immer hör' ich's rauschen:
Du fändest Ruhe dort!
Du fändest Ruhe dort!

5. The Linden Tree

A linden tree is standing
beside a flowing stream,
And here beneath its branches
I dreamed my sweetest dream.

I carved her name into its bark,
And loving words so dear,
And in my joy and sorrow
It always drew me here.

And now I must pass by it,
Pass by in deepest night,
And even in the darkness
I keep it from my sight.

I hear its branches rustle,
And call as I go past;
"Come here to me my brother
And find your peace at last".

The bitter wind is whistling,
So cold into my face,
My hat flies off behind me,
I dare not slow my pace.

I've walked for many hours now,
And still its call I hear,
The rustling of its branches,
"You'll find a haven here".

I've walked for many hours now,
And still its call I hear,
The rustling of its branches,
"you'll find a haven here",
"you'll find a haven here".

6. Wasserflut

Manche Trän' aus meinen Augen
ist gefallen in den Schnee;
seine kalten Flocken saugen
durstig ein das heiße Weh,
durstig ein das heiße Weh.

Wenn die Gräser sprossen wollen
weht daher ein lauer Wind,
und das Eis zerspringt in Schollen
und der weiche Schnee zerrinnt,
und der weiche Schnee zerrinnt.

Schnee, du weißt von meinem Sehnen,
Sag' mir, wohin doch geht dein Lauf?
Folge nach nur meinen Tränen,
nimmt dich bald das Bächlein auf,
nimmt dich bald das Bächlein auf.

Wirst mit ihm die Stadt durchziehen,
munt're Straßen ein und aus;
Fühlst du meine Tränen glühen,
da ist meiner Liebsten Haus.
da ist meiner Liebsten Haus.

6. Rushing Water

From my eyes the tears are falling,
Tears I can no more restrain.
And the snow engulfs my anguish,
Thirstily drinks my burning pain,
Thirstily drinks my burning pain.

When the grass again is growing
And the wind is warm once more,
Then the ice will soon be flowing
And the snow will start to thaw,
And the snow will start to thaw.

Snow you know of my longing,
where you go will you not say!
If you follow my teardrops.
Soon the stream will take you away,
Soon the stream will take you away.

To the town you will soon be turning,
winding through each street and close.
When you feel my tears are burning,
there is my beloved's house,
there is my beloved's house.

7. Auf dem Flusse

Der du so lustig rauschtest,
du heller, wilder Fluß,
wie still bist du geworden,
gibst keinen Scheidegruß.

Mit harter, starrer Rinde
hast du dich überdeckt,
liegst kalt und unbeweglich
im Sande ausgestreckt.

In deine Decke grab' ich
mit einem spitzen Stein
den Namen meiner Liebsten
und Stund und Tag hinein:

Den Tag des ersten Grußes,
den Tag, an dem ich ging;
um Nam' und Zahlen windet
Sich ein zerbrochner Ring.

Mein Herz, in diesem Bache
erkennst du nun dein Bild?
Ob's unter seiner Rinde
Wohl auch so reißend schwillt?
Ob's wohl auch so reißend schwillt?
Mein Herz, in diesem Bache
erkennst du nun dein Bild?
Ob's unter seiner Rinde
Wohl auch so reißend schwillt?
Ob's wohl auch so reißend schwillt?
Ob's wohl auch so reißend schwillt?

7. By the Stream

Are you the same bright river
That gaily rushed along?
How still you are and silent,
No greeting in your song.

You are no longer rushing,
your surface hard and sealed.
How cold you lie, unmoving,
Outstretched across the field.

I'll cut into your surface
The name I can't forget,
The name of my beloved,
The day and hour we met.

That day of our first meeting,
The day we had to part,
Her name, and time, then round it all
I'll carve a broken heart.

My heart, within this river
you see yourself so well,
Beneath Its Icy cover
The raging torrents swell,
Ah, the raging torrents swell.
My heart within this river
you see yourself so well,
Beneath Its Icy cover
The raging torrents swell,
Ah, the raging torrents swell,
Ah, the raging torrents swell.

8. Rückblick

Es brennt mir unter beiden Sohlen,
Tret' ich auch schon auf Eis und Schnee,
Ich möcht' nicht wieder Atem holen,
Bis ich nicht mehr die Türme seh'.

Hab' mich an jeden Stein gestoßen,
so eilt' ich zu der Stadt hinaus;
die Krähen warfen Bäll' und
    Schloßen
auf meinen Hut von jedem Haus,
die Krähen warfen Bäll' und
    Schloßen
auf meinen Hut von jedem Haus.

Wie anders hast du mich empfangen,
du Stadt der Unbeständigkeit!
An deinen blanken Fenstern sangen
die Lerch' und Nachtigall im Streit.

Die runden Lindenbäume
    blühten,
die klaren Rinnen rauschten
    hell,
und ach, zwei Mädchenaugen glühten.
Da war's gescheh'n um dich, Gesell'!
und ach, zwei Mädchenaugen glühten.
Da war's gescheh'n um dich, Gesell'!

Kömmt mir der Tag in die Gedanken,
möcht' ich noch einmal rückwärts seh'n,
möcht' ich zurücke wieder wanken,
vor ihrem Hause stille steh'n.

Kömmt mir der Tag in die Gedanken,
möcht' ich noch einmal rückwärts seh'n,
möcht' ich zurücke wieder wanken,
vor ihrem Hause stille steh'n.
möcht' ich zurücke wieder wanken,
vor ihrem Hause stille steh'n,
vor ihrem Hause stille steh'n.

8. Backwards Glance

I wonder why my feet are burning,
Although I walk on ice and snow.
I want my breath to cease within me
Until the roofs no longer show.

I bruise myself on every boulder,
The town I leave is still too close,
The crows were throwing snow and
    hailstones
Upon my head from every house,
The crows were throwing snow and
    hailstones
Upon my head from every house.

How different were you at our meeting,
Oh fickle town you welcomed me!
The larks and nightingales were singing
Before your windows cheerfully.

The breeze through linden flowers
    blowing,
The clear streams rushing round each
    bend,
And ah, the maiden's eyes were glowing,
It's then you lost your heart my friend,
And ah, the maiden's eyes were glowing,
It's then you lost your heart my friend.

I think of days before we parted,
I'm longing to look back once more,
To stumble back to where I started
And stand again before her door.

I think of days before we parted,
I'm longing to look back once more,
To stumble back to where I started
And stand again before her door.
I'm longing to look back once more,
Just to stand again before her door,
And stand again before her door.

9. Irrlicht

In die tiefsten Felsengründe
lockte mich ein Irrlicht hin:
Wie ich einen Ausgang finde,
liegt nicht schwer mir in dem Sinn,
liegt nicht schwer mir in dem Sinn.

Bin gewohnt das Irregehen,
's führt ja jeder Weg zum Ziel:
Unsre Freuden, unsre Wehen,
alles eines Irrlichts Spiel!
alles eines Irrlichts Spiel!

Durch des Bergstroms trock'ne Rinnen
wind' ich ruhig mich hinab,
jeder Strom wird's Meer gewinnen,
jedes Leiden auch ein Grab,
jeder Strom wird's Meer gewinnen,
jedes Leiden auch ein Grab.

9. Will-o'-the-Wisp

In the deepest rocky cavern,
A Will-o'-the-Wisp has lured me there.
How I'll ever find my way now,
In my heart I do not care,
In my heart I do not care.

I'm so used to being lost now,
Every pathway has its aims.
All our joys and all our sorrows,
All are Will-o'-the-Wisp's own games,
All are Will-o'-the-Wisp's own games.

Through the mountain streams dry bed I walk,
Turning every winding bend.
Every stream must reach the ocean,
Every sorrow has its end.
Every stream must reach the ocean,
Every sorrow has its end.

10. Rast

Nun merk' ich erst, wie müd' ich bin,
da ich zur Ruh' mich lege:
das Wandern hielt mich munter hin
auf unwirtbarem Wege.

Die Füße frugen nicht nach Rast,
es war zu kalt zum Stehen;
der Rücken fühlte keine Last,
der Sturm half fort mich wehen,
der Rücken fühlte keine Last,
der Sturm half fort mich wehen.

In eines Köhlers engem Haus
hab' Obdach ich gefunden;
doch meine Glieder ruh'n nicht aus:
So brennen ihre Wunden.

Auch du, mein Herz, in Kampf und Sturm
so wild und so verwegen,
fühlst in der Still' erst deinen Wurm
mit heißem Stich sich regen!
fühlst in der Still' erst deinen Wurm
mit heißem Stich sich regen!

10. Rest

I'm now aware how tired I am,
As I lie down so weary:
The wandering kept me awake
On pathways cold and dreary.

And yet my feet did not seek rest,
To stand in freezing weather.
The raging storm upon my back
Just helped to drive me further,
The raging storm upon my back
Just helped to drive me further.

I've found a charcoal burner's hut
The weary traveller uses,
But yet my aching limbs rest not
From all my burning bruises.

You too, my heart, in strife and storm,
So wild and so unyielding,
Within its stillness feel the serpent writhe,
Its sting so fiercely burning!
Within its stillness feel the serpent writhe,
Its sting so fiercely burning!

11. Frühlingstraum

Ich träumte von bunten Blumen,
So wie sie wohl blühen im Mai;
Ich träumte von grünen Wiesen,
Von lustigem Vogelgeschrei
Von lustigem Vogelgeschrei.

Und als die Hähne krähten,
Da ward mein Auge wach;
Da war es kalt und finster,
Es schrieen die Raben vom Dach,
Da war es kalt und finster,
Es schrieen die Raben vom Dach.

Doch an den Fensterscheiben,
Wer malte die Blätter da?
Doch an den Fensterscheiben,
Wer malte die Blätter da?
Ihr lacht wohl über den Träumer,
Der Blumen im Winter sah?
Der Blumen im Winter sah?

Ich träumte von Lieb' um Liebe,
Von einer schönen Maid,
Von Herzen und von Küssen,
Von Wonn' und Seligkeit,
Von Wonn' und Seligkeit.

Und als die Hähne kräten,
Da ward mein Herze wach;
Nun sitz ich hier alleine
Und denke dem Traume nach,
Nun sitz ich hier alleine
Und denke dem Traume nach.

11. Dreams of Spring

I dreamt of the brightest flowers,
That bloom in the warmth of the spring;
I dreamt of the green meadows,
Where merry birds noisily sing,
Where merry birds noisily sing.

And then the cocks were crowing,
I woke to end my dream;
And in the freezing darkness
I heard the ravens scream,
And in the freezing darkness
I heard the ravens scream.

But on the frosty window,
Who painted the leafy spray?
But on the frosty window,
Who painted that leafy spray?
You laugh perhaps at the dreamer,
For seeing the flowers of May,
For dreaming of flowers of May.

I dreamt of love and loving,
One girl of such loveliness,
I dreamt of hearts and kisses,
Of joy and happiness,
Of joy and of happiness.

And then the cocks were crowing.
My heart awoke again;
I sat alone in silence
And tried to recall my dream,
I sat alone in silence
And tried to recall my dream.

Die Augen schließ' ich wieder,	My eyelids close in slumber,
Noch schlägt das Herz so warm,	My heart still beats so warm,
Die Augen schließ' ich wieder,	My eyelids close in slumber,
Noch schlägt das Herz so warm.	Still beats my heart so warm.
Wann grünt ihr Blätter am Fenster?	And when green leaves shade the window,
Wann halt' ich mein Liebchen im Arm?	Shall I hold my love in my arms?
Wann halt' ich mein Liebchen im Arm?	Will she be once more in my arms?

12. Einsamkeit

Wie eine trübe Wolke
durch heit're Lüfte geht,
wenn in der Tanne Wipfel
ein mattes Lüftchen weht:

So zieh ich meine Straße
dahin mit trägem Fuß,
durch helles, frohes Leben,
einsam und ohne Gruß.

Ach, daß die Luft so ruhig!
Ach, daß die Welt so licht!
Als noch die Stürme tobten,
war ich so elend, so elend nicht,
Ach, daß die Luft so ruhig!
Ach, daß die Welt so licht!
Als noch die Stürme tobten,
war ich so elend, so elend nicht.

12. Solitude

How like a cloud above me
Which sails through clear blue skies,
When in the tops of pine trees
A gentle breeze will rise.

So like that cloud I wander
With weary trudging feet,
Through life that's bright and cheerful,
Alone, no-one to greet.

Ah, why a day so peaceful?
Ah, why a world so fresh?
When all the storms were raging,
I never knew such wretchedness,
Ah, why a day so peaceful?
Ah, why a world so fresh?
When all the storms were raging,
I never knew such wretchedness.

13. Die Post

Von der Straße her ein Posthorn
 klingt.
Was hat es, daß es so hoch
 aufspringt,
mein Herz?
Was hat es, daß es so hoch
 aufspringt,
mein Herz? mein Herz?

Die Post bringt keinen Brief für dich.
Was drängst du denn so wunderlich,
mein Herz? mein Herz?
Die Post bringt keinen Brief für dich,
mein Herz? mein Herz?
Was drängst du denn so wunderlich,
mein Herz? mein Herz?

Nun ja, die Post kömmt aus der Stadt,
wo ich ein liebes Liebchen hatt',
mein Herz!
wo ich ein liebes Liebchen hatt',
mein Herz! mein Herz!

Willst wohl einmal hinüberseh'n
und fragen, wie es dort mag geh'n,
mein Herz? mein Herz?
Willst wohl einmal hinüberseh'n
mein Herz? mein Herz?
und fragen, wie es dort mag geh'n,
mein Herz? mein Herz?

13. The Mail Coach

From the highway hear the post horn
 sound.
What makes you suddenly leap and
 pound,
My heart?
What makes you suddenly leap and
 pound,
My heart? my heart?

The coach for me no note will bring.
What urged you then to leap and sing,
My heart? my heart?
The coach for me no note will bring,
My heart? my heart?
What urged you then to leap and sing,
My heart? my heart?

Ah yes, the mail coach leaves the town,
Where once the sweetest love I'd known,
My heart!
Where once the sweetest love I'd known,
My heart! my heart!

Perhaps to look back once again
And ask the question 'Who's to blame?',
My heart? my heart?
Perhaps to look back once again,
My heart? my heart?
And ask the question 'Who's to blame?',
My heart? my heart?

14. Der greise Kopf

Der Reif hatt' einen weißen Schein
mir übers Haar gestreuet;
da glaubt' ich schon ein Greis zu sein
Und hab' mich sehr gefreuet.

Doch bald ist er hinweggetaut,
hab' wieder schwarze Haare,
daß mir's vor meiner Jugend graut
wie weit noch bis zur Bahre!
wie weit noch bis zur Bahre!

Vom Abendrot zum Morgenlicht
ward mancher Kopf zum Greise.
Wer glaubt's? und meiner ward es nicht
auf dieser ganzen Reise!
auf dieser ganzen Reise!

14. The Grey Head

A freezing mist with ghostly shine
Upon my hair alighted;
If I was old before my time
Then I would be delighted.

But soon the frost began to thaw,
Black hair returned to haunt me,
I shuddered at my youth once more,
My grave how long you taunt me!
My grave how long you taunt me!

From setting sun to morning light
So many heads have turned to grey.
Who'd think that mine has not turned white
On all this winter's journey!
On all this winter's journey!

15. Die Krähe

Eine Krähe war mit mir
Aus der Stadt gezogen,
Ist bis heute für und für
Um mein Haupt geflogen.

Krähe, wunderliches Tier,
Willst mich nicht verlassen?
Meinst wohl, bald als Beute hier
Meinen Leib zu fassen?

Nun, es wird nicht weit mehr geh'n
An dem Wanderstabe.
Krähe, laß mich endlich seh'n,
Treue bis zum Grabe!
Krähe, laß mich endlich seh'n,
Treue bis zum Grabe!

15. The Crow

I was followed by a crow
From the village trailing,
All day flying to and fro
Round my head still sailing.

Crow, fascinating crow,
Endlessly you tease me,
Thinking of the prey below,
Watching when to seize me.

Now I have not far to go,
Carry me no more my stave.
Crow, Oh crow, then show to me,
Faith until the grave!
Crow, Oh crow, then show to me,
Faith until the grave!

16. Letzte Hoffnung

Hie und da ist an den Bäumen
manches bunte Blatt zu seh'n,
und ich bleibe vor den Bäumen
oftmals in Gedanken steh'n.

Schaue nach dem einen Blatte,
hänge meine Hoffnung dran;
spielt der Wind mit meinem Blatte,
zittr' ich, was ich zittern kann.

Ach, und fällt das Blatt zu Boden,
fällt mit ihm die Hoffnung ab;
fall' ich selber mit zu Boden,
wein, wein' auf meiner Hoffnung
   Grab.
wein' auf meiner Hoffnung
   Grab.

16. The Last Hope

Here and there on frozen branches
Autumn leaves can still be seen,
And I stand in silence, thinking,
Watching them as in a dream.

At a single leaf I'm gazing,
On it all my hopes are pinned;
And I tremble while I'm watching,
As it's played with by the wind.

If it falls it soon will perish,
With it all my hopes as well;
So I fall on hopes I cherish,
Weep, weep, oh weep on my hope's
   grave,
Weep, weep, oh weep on my hope's
   grave.

17. Im Dorfe

Es bellen die Hunde,
es rascheln die Ketten;
es schlafen die Menschen in ihren Betten,
träumen sich manches, was sie nicht haben,
tun sich im Guten und Argen erlaben:
Und morgen früh ist alles zerflossen.

Je nun, Je nun, sie haben ihr Teil genossen,
und hoffen, und hoffen,
was sie noch übrig ließen,
doch wieder zu finden, doch wieder zu finden,
auf ihren Kissen.

Bellt mich nur fort, ihr wachen Hunde,
laßt mich nicht ruh'n in der Schlummerstunde!
Ich bin zu Ende mit allen Träumen
was will ich unter den Schläfern säumen?
Ich bin zu Ende mit allen Träumen
was will ich unter den Schläfern säumen?

17. In the Village

The watchdogs are barking,
Their chain-links are rattling,
And folk are asleep, In their beds they are settling,
Dreaming of having things they're not able,
Finding their pleasures in both good and evil:
And in the morning all dreams have vanished.

Ah well, Ah well, their dreams have been full of pleasure,
And hoping, and hoping,
That some dreams they may still treasure,
And maybe a new dream, remains on their pillows,
Upon their pillows.

Drive me away, as watch you are keeping,
Give me no rest in the hours of sleeping!
My dreams are ended, I need them no longer,
Why should I stay where the dreamers linger?
My dreams are ended, I need dreams no longer,
Why should I stay where the dreamers linger?

18. Der stümische Morgen

Wie hat der Sturm zerrissen
des Himmels graues Kleid!
Die Wolkenfetzen flattern
umher im matten Streit,
umher im matten Streit.

Und rote Feuerflammen
zieh'n zwischen ihnen hin;
Das nenn' ich einen Morgen
so recht nach meinem Sinn!
Mein Herz sieht an dem Himmel
gemalt sein eig'nes Bild –
es ist nichts als der Winter,
es ist nichts als der Winter,
der Winter, kalt und wild!

18. The Stormy Morning

How fierce the storm is rending
The dark grey clouds on high,
The tattered clouds are swirling
Around the weary sky,
Around the weary sky.

And red the sky is flaming
Through clouds in flying haste;
This really is a morning
That's suited to my taste,
And in the sky is painted
My image clear and bold,
It's nothing but the winter,
It's nothing but the winter,
The winter wild and cold!

19. Täuschung

Ein Licht tanzt freundlich vor mir her,
ich folg' ihm nach die Kreuz und Quer;
ich folg' ihm gern und seh's ihm an,
daß es verlockt den Wandersmann.
Ach! wer wie ich so elend ist,
gibt gern sich hin der bunten List,
die hinter Eis und Nacht und Graus
ihm weist ein helles, warmes
   Haus.
und eine liebe Seele drin
nur Täuschung ist für mich Gewinn!

19. Illusion

I see a friendly dancing light,
I follow, keeping it in sight;
I'll follow it so willingly,
Although it tempts me from my way.
Ah, they who know my wretched plight
Would gladly fall for dazzling light,
Where ends the night, and cold and fear,
And shows a house with warmth and
   cheer,
And someone waiting at the door,
But it's illusion just once more.

20. Der Wegweiser

Was vermeid' ich denn die Wege,
wo die ander'n Wand'rer gehn,
suche mir versteckte Stege
durch verschneite Felsenhöh'n?
suche mir versteckte Stege
durch verschneite Felsenhöh'n?
durch Felsenhöh'n?

Habe ja doch nichts begangen,
daß ich Menschen sollte scheu'n,
daß ich Menschen sollte scheu'n,
welch ein törichtes Verlangen
treibt mich in die Wüstenei'n?
treibt mich in die Wüstenei'n?

Weiser stehen auf den Strassen,
weisen auf die Städte zu,
und ich wand're sonder Maßen
ohne Ruh' und suche Ruh'
und ich wand're sonder Maßen
ohne Ruh' und suche Ruh',
nd suche Ruh'.

Einen Weiser seh' ich stehen
unverrückt vor meinem Blick;
eine Straße muß ich gehen,
eine Straße muß ich gehen,
die noch keiner ging zurück.

Einen Weiser seh' ich stehen
unverrückt vor meinem Blick;
eine Straße muß ich gehen,
die noch keiner ging zurück,
die noch keiner ging zurück.

20. The Signpost

Why do I avoid the pathways
which the other travellers use?
It's the snow-capped hills I'm seeking,
It's the hidden paths I choose,
It's the snow-capped hills I'm seeking,
It's the hidden paths I choose,
Hidden paths I choose.

I have done no wrong to others,
Why should I then shun mankind?
Why should I then shun mankind?
So what is this foolish longing
Driving me to distant land?
Driving me to distant land?

Signposts to the towns are pointing,
Shall I go where they suggest?
Shall I wander on regardless,
without rest, yet seeking rest?
Shall I wander on regardless,
without rest, yet seeking rest?
Yet seeking rest?

I see only one clear signpost
Pointing to my lonely track;
It's the road which I must travel,
It's the road which I must travel,
From which no-one can come back.

I see only one clear signpost
Pointing to my lonely track;
It's the road which I must travel,
From which no-one can come back,
From which no-one can come back.

21. Das Wirtshaus

Auf einen Totenacker
hat mich mein Weg gebracht;
Allhier will ich einkehren,
hab' ich bei mir gedacht.

Ihr grünen Totenkränze
könnt wohl die Zeichen sein,
die müde Wand'rer laden
ins kühle Wirtshaus ein.

Sind denn in diesem Hause
die Kammern all' besetzt?
Bin matt zum Niedersinken,
bin tödlich schwer verletzt.

O unbarmherz'ge Schenke,
doch weisest du mich ab?
Nun weiter denn, nur weiter,
mein treuer Wanderstab!
Nun weiter denn, nur weiter,
mein treuer Wanderstab!

21. The Inn

Into a silent graveyard
My journey now has led;
So here I will take refuge,
And lay my weary head.

The funeral wreaths might well be
The tavern's welcome signs,
Inviting weary travellers
Into its cool confines.

Has every room been taken?
Are all already used?
With weariness I'm sinking,
How painfully I'm bruised.

Oh cruel and heartless tavern,
Why do you drive me off?
Then onward, only onward,
My true and trusty staff,
Then onward, only onward,
My true and trusty staff.

22. Mut!

Fliegt der Schnee mir ins Gesicht,
schüttl' ich ihn herunter.
Wenn mein Herz im Busen spricht,
sing' ich hell und munter.

Höre nicht, was es mir sagt,
habe keine Ohren;
fühle nicht, was es mir klagt,
Klagen ist für Toren.

Lustig in die Welt hinein
gegen Wind und Wetter!
Will kein Gott auf Erden sein,
sind wir selber Götter!

Lustig in die Welt hinein
gegen Wind und Wetter!
Will kein Gott auf Erden sein,
sind wir selber Götter!

22. Courage!

Snow is flying in my face,
I just shake it from me.
When my heart cries in distress,
I just sing more brightly.

Do not hear my heart's lament,
Close your ears to whining;
Do not feel its discontent,
Fools are always pining.

Stride then gaily through the world
Braving wind and weather!
If there are no Gods on earth,
Gods we will be together.

Stride then gaily through the world
Braving wind and weather!
If there are no Gods on earth,
Gods we will be together.

23. Die Nebensonnen

Drei Sonnen sah ich am Himmel steh'n,
hab' lang und fest sie angeseh'n;
und sie auch standen da so stier,
als könnten sie nicht weg von mir.

Ach, meine Sonnen seid ihr nicht!
Schaut Andren doch ins Angesicht!
Ja, neulich hatt' ich auch wohl drei;
nun sind hinab die besten zwei.
Ging nur die dritt' erst hinterdrein!
Im Dunkeln wird mir wohler sein.

23. The Mock Suns

I saw three suns in the heaven's haze,
I stared at them with a steady gaze;
They also stayed so still above,
As if from me they would not move.

Ah, my own suns you cannot be!
At others stare, but not at me,
Yes, I had three not long since past;
Now one remains, the best two lost,
If only now the third would flee,
The darkness would be best for me.

24. Der Leiermann

Drüben hinterm Dorfe
steht ein Leiermann
und mit starren Fingern
dreht er, was er kann.

Barfuß auf dem Eise
wankt er hin und her
und sein kleiner Teller
bleibt ihm immer leer,
und sein kleiner Teller
bleibt ihm immer leer.

Keiner mag ihn hören,
keiner sieht ihn an,
und die Hunde knurren
um den alten Mann.

Und er läßt es gehen
alles, wie es will,
dreht und seine Leier
steht ihm nimmer still,
dreht und seine Leier
steht ihm nimmer still.

Wunderlicher Alter,
soll ich mit dir geh'n?
Willst zu meinen Liedern
deine Leier dreh'n?

24. The Organ Grinder

Just beyond the town
An organ grinder stands,
And he turns the handle
With his frozen hands.

Barefoot in the snow
He shuffles on his way,
Not a single penny
In his empty tray,
Not a single penny
In his empty tray.

No-one wants to hear him,
No-one looks his way.
Dogs are snarling round him,
No heed does he pay.

But he lets it happen
As it always will,
He just goes on turning,
Never is he still,
He just goes on turning,
Never is he still.

Curious old fellow,
Shall I go along?
Will you grind your organ
Only to my song?

Franz Schubert

Schwanengesang – Swan Song

Schwanengesang (Swan Song), D 957, is a collection of fourteen songs written by Franz Schubert at the end of his life and published posthumously.

Named by it's first publisher, Tobias Haslinger, who no doubt wished to present it as Schubert's last composition, *Schwanengesang* is different from the preceding *Die schöne Müllerin* and *Die Winterreise* song cycles by including settings of more than one poet. Seven texts by Ludwig Rellstab (1799–1860) are followed by six by Heinrich Heine (1797–1856); inclusion of the last song, to words by Johann Gabriel Seidl (1804–1875), may or may not align with the desires and intentions of Schubert. In any case, all fourteen songs were composed in 1828 and the collection was published in 1829, a short time after the composer's death.

The Rellstab and Heine settings were copied in a single sitting on consecutive pages of the manuscript in Schubert's hand, and Seidl's *Die Taubenpost* is thought to be Schubert's last Lied — hence the foundation for Haslinger's progression, one accepted by history together with his idea that a cycle exists at all (the true cycles *Die schöne Müllerin* and *Die Winterreise* had sold well, encouraging the publisher). The title *Schwanengesang* is not of course the composer's but all the song titles are; Heine, for one, did not name his poems.

1. Liebesbotschaft

Rauschendes Bächlein, so silbern und hell,
Eilst zur Geliebten so munter und schnell?
Ach, trautes Bächlein, mein Bote sei du;
Bringe die Grüsse des Fernen ihr zu.

All' ihre Blumen im Garten gepflegt,
Die sie so lieblich am Busen trägt,
Und ihre Rosen in purpurner Glut,
Bächlein, erquicke mit kühlender Flut,
Und ihre Rosen in purpurner Glut,
Bächlein, erquicke mit kühlender Flut.

Wenn sie am Ufer, in Träume versenkt,
Meiner gedenkend, das Köpfchen hängt;
Tröste die Süsse mit freundlichem Blick,
Denn der Geliebte kehrt bald zurück,
Tröste die Süsse mit freundlichem Blick,
Denn der Geliebte kehrt bald zurück.

Neigt sich die Sonne mit rötlichem Schein,
Wiege das Liebchen in Schlummer ein.
Rausche sie murmelnd in süsse Ruh,
Flüstre ihr Träume der Liebe zu,
Flüstre ihr Träume der Liebe zu.

1. Love's Message

Rush little streamlet so silver and bright
To my sweet love will you race with delight
Ah, little streamlet, my messenger dear
Carry my greetings to one far from here.

All of her flowers which she tends and prepares
And at her breast so charmingly wears
And on her roses with rich crimson glow
Spray your cool ripples as you quickly flow,
And on her roses with rich crimson glow
Spray your cool ripples as quickly you flow.

When on your banks, lost in dreams she will be
Little head drooping, she thinks of me
Comfort the sweet one who waits there alone
From your kind glance she will know I'll be home,
Comfort the sweet one who waits there alone
From your kind glance she will know I'll be home.

And with the sun sinking low in the west
Cradle my sweetheart so she may rest
Ripple and murmur so sleep will ensue
Whisper the love dreams I send with you,
Whisper the love dreams I send with you.

2. Kriegers Ahnung

In tiefer Ruh liegt um mich her
Der Waffenbrüder Kreis;
Mir ist das Herz so bang und schwer,
so bang, und schwer,
Von Sehnsucht mir so heiss,
Von Sehnsucht mir so heiss.

Wie hab' ich oft so süss geträumt
An ihrem Busen warm,
An ihrem Busen warm!
Wie freundlich schien des Herdes Glut,
Lag sie in meinem Arm,
Lag sie in meinem Arm!

Hier, wo der Flammen düstrer
 Schein
Ach! nur auf Waffen spielt,
Hier fühlt die Brust sich ganz allein,
Hier fühlt die Brust sich ganz allein,
Der Wehmut Träne quillt,
Der Wehmut Träne quillt.

Herz! Dass der Trost Dich nicht
 verlässt,
Dass der Trost Dich nicht verlässt!
Es ruft noch manche Schlacht
Bald ruh ich wohl und schlafe
 fest,
Herzliebste, Gute Nacht!
Herzliebste, Gute Nacht!
Herz! Dass der Trost Dich nicht
 verlässt,
Dass der Trost Dich nicht verlässt!
Es ruft noch manche Schlacht.
Bald ruh ich wohl und schlafe
 fest,
Herzliebste, Gute Nacht!
Herzliebste, Gute Nacht!
Herzliebste, Gute Nacht!

2. The Soldier's Foreboding

In deepest sleep around me
My comrades lie unseen
My heavy heart sighs wearily
Sighs wearily
From longing how I burn,
From longing how I burn.

How often did I sweetly dream
Upon her breasts so warm,
Upon her breasts so warm
How friendly did the firelight gleam
As she lay in my arms,
As she lay in my arms.

Here where the flames have all died
 down
Ah, only weapons gleam
My aching heart feels so alone,
My aching heart feels so alone
Sad tears being to stream,
Sad tears being to stream.

Heart may your hopes with you
 remain,
May your hopes with you remain
Throughout the call to fight
Soon peace will come and I shall sleep
 again
My dearest love, goodnight
My dearest, now goodnight.
Heart may your hopes with you
 remain,
May your hopes with you remain
Throughout the call to fight
Soon peace will come and I shall sleep
 again
My dearest love, goodnight,
My dearest, now goodnight,
My dearest, now goodnight.

3. Frühlingssehnsucht

Säuselnde Lüfte wehend so mild,
Blumiger Düfte atmend erfüllt!
Säuselnde Lüfte wehend so mild,
Blumiger Düfte atmend erfüllt!
Wie haucht ihr mich wonnig
  begrüssend an!
Wie habt ihr dem pochenden Herzen
  getan?
Es möchte euch folgen auf luftiger
  Bahn,
Es möchte euch folgen auf luftiger
  Bahn,
Wohin? Wohin?

Bächlein, so munter rauschend zumal,
Wollen hinunter silbern in's Tal.
Bächlein, so munter rauschend zumal,
Wollen hinunter silbern in's Tal.
Die schwebende Welle, dort eilt sie
  dahin!
Tief spiegeln sich Fluren und Himmel
  darin.
Was ziehst du mich, sehnend
  verlangender Sinn,
Was ziehst du mich, sehnend
  verlangender Sinn,
Hinab? Hinab?

Grüssender Sonne spielendes Gold,
Hoffende Wonne bringest du hold.
Grüssender Sonne spielendes Gold,
Hoffende Wonne bringest du hold.
Wie labt mich dein selig begrüssendes
  Bild!
Es lächelt am tiefblauen Himmel so
  mild
Und hat mir das Auge mit Tränen
  gefüllt!
Und hat mir das Auge mit Tränen
  gefüllt!

3. Spring Longing

Whispering breezes gently they blow
Breathing the scent of flowers as they go,
Whispering breezes gently they blow
Breathing the scent of flowers as they go
How sweetly you greet me with softest
  voice
My heart throbs so fast, with each beat
  I rejoice
I'd like to go with you to follow your
  course,
I'd like to go with you to follow your
  course
Oh where, oh where.

Fast little streamlet, rush on your way
Flow down the dale with silvery spray
Fast little streamlet, rush on your way
Flow down the dale with silvery spray
The shimmering ripples are seeming
  to fly
Reflecting the meadows and blue of the
  sky
Why do you invite me with yearning
  desire,
Why do you invite me with yearning
  desire
And down, and down.

Welcoming sunbeams shining like gold
Seeing the bliss you bring us unfold
Welcoming sunbeams shining like gold
Seeing the bliss you bring us unfold
How warmly I'm blessed as above me
  you rise
You smile at me softly from deepest blue
  skies
So why are there tears flowing into my
  eyes?
So why are the tears flowing into my
  eyes?

Warum? Warum?	Oh why? oh why?
Grünend umkränzet Wälder und Höh'!	Green crowns the woods and hills everywhere
Schimmernd erglänzet Blütenschnee.	Blossoms like snowflakes glint in the air,
Grünend umkränzet Wälder und Höh'!	Green crowns the woods and hills everywhere
Schimmernd erglänzet Blütenschnee.	Blossoms like snowflakes glint in the air
So dränget sich alles zum bräutlichen Licht;	And all things are drawn to the virginal light
Es schwellen die Keime, die Knospe bricht;	The swelling of buds and the seeds taking flight
Sie haben gefunden, was ihnen gebricht,	And from their achievement they take such delight
Sie haben gefunden, was ihnen gebricht:	And from their achievement they take such delight
Und du? Und du?	And you? and you?
Rastloses Sehnen! Wünschendes Herz,	Restless desire and longing remain
Immer nur Tränen, Klage und Schmerz?	Always the weeping, heartache and pain,
Rastloses Sehnen! Wünschendes Herz,	Restless desire and longing remain
Immer nur Tränen, Klage und Schmerz?	Always the weeping, heartache and pain
Auch ich bin mir schwellender Triebe bewusst!	I too can be driven by rising new zest
Wer stillet mir endlich die drängende Lust?	Whoever can end the desire and brings rest
Nur du befreist den Lenz in der Brust,	Just you can free the youth in my breast
Nur du befreist den Lenz in der Brust,	Just you can free the youth in my breast
Nur du! Nur du!	Just you, just you.

4. Ständchen

Leise flehen meine Lieder
Durch die Nacht zu Dir;
In den stillen Hain hernieder,
Liebchen, komm' zu mir!

Flüsternd schlanke Wipfel rauschen
In des Mondes Licht,
In des Mondes Licht;
Des Verräters feindlich Lauschen
Fürchte, Holde, nicht,
Fürchte, Holde, nicht.

Hörst die Nachtigallen schlagen?
Ach! sie flehen Dich,
Mit der Töne süssen Klagen
Flehen sie für mich.

Sie verstehn des Busens Sehnen,
Kennen Liebesschmerz,
Kennen Liebesschmerz,
Rühren mit den Silbertönen
Jedes weiche Herz,
Jedes weiche Herz.

Lass auch Dir die Brust bewegen,
Liebchen, höre mich!
Bebend harr' ich Dir entgegen!
Komm', beglücke mich!
Komm', beglücke mich,
beglücke mich!

4. Serenade

Can you hear my song entreating
Softly through the night
In the silent glade I'm waiting
Come to me my sweet.

Slender treetops whisper near us
Where the moonbeams shine
Where the moonbeams shine
No-one will betray or hear us
Fear not, love of mine,
Fear not, love of mine.

Nightingales my songs are pressing
Ah, imploring you
With their sweet lament caressing
They implore you too.

They know all the heartfelt yearning
All the loving hurt,
All the loving hurt
Every silvery tone is stirring
Each gentle heart,
Each gentle heart.

Let you heart be moved by passion
Sweetheart hear my plea
Trembling I await compassion
Come bring joy to me,
Come bring joy to me,
Come bring me joy!

5. Aufenthalt

Rauschender Strom, brausender Wald,
Starrender Fels mein Aufenthalt,
Rauschender Strom, brausender Wald,
Starrender Fels mein Aufenthalt.
Wie sich die Welle an Welle reiht,
Fliessen die Tränen mir ewig erneut,
Fliessen die Tränen mir ewig, ewig erneut,
Fliessen die Tränen mir ewig erneut.

Hoch in den Kronen wogend sich's regt,
So unaufhörlich mein Herze schlägt,
Hoch in den Kronen wogend sich's regt,
So unaufhörlich mein Herze schlägt,
So unaufhörlich mein Herze schlägt.
Und wie des Felsen uraltes Erz
Ewig deselbe bleibet mein Schmerz,
Ewig deselbe bleibet, bleibet mein Schmerz,
Ewig deselbe bleibet mein Schmerz.

Rauschender Strom, brausender Wald,
Starrender Fels mein Aufenthalt,
Rauschender Strom, brausender Wald,
Starrender Fels, Rauschender Strom,
brausender Wald mein Aufenthalt.

5. Resting Place

Forest so wild, rivers that race
Menacing rocks, my resting place.
Forest so wild, rivers that race
Menacing rocks, my resting place.
Storm waters surging the endless flood
Flow as my tears flow, forever renewed
Flow as my tears flow, and ever, ever renewed
Flow as my tears flow, forever renewed

Just as the treetops are stirred by the wind
To endless pounding my heart is resigned
Just as the treetops are stirred by the wind
To endless pounding my heart is resigned.
To endless pounding my heart is resigned
As ancient stone always stays the same
Grief never ending fills me with pain
Grief never ending fills me, fills me with pain
Grief never ending fills me with pain.

Forest so wild, rivers that race
Menacing rocks, my resting place.
Forest so wild, rivers that race
Menacing rocks, rivers that race
Forest so wild, my resting place.

6. In der Ferne

Wehe dem Fliehenden
Welt hinaus ziehenden! –
Fremde durchmessenden,
Heimat vergessenden,
Mutterhaus hassenden,
Freunde verlassenden
Folget kein Segen,
Ach! Auf ihren Wegen nach,
Auf ihren Wegen nach!

Herze, das sehnende,
Auge, das tränende,
Sehnsucht, nie endende,
Heimwärts sich wendende!
Busen, der wallende,
Klage, verhallende,
Abendstern, blinkender,
Hoffnungslos sinkender,
Hoffnungslos sinkender!

Lüfte, ihr säuselnden,
Wellen, sanft kräuselnden,
Sonnenstrahl, eilender,
Nirgend verweilender:
Die mir mit Schmerze, ach!
Dies treue Herze brach –
Grüsst von dem Fliehenden
Welt hinaus ziehenden,
Welt hinaus ziehenden!

Lüfte, ihr säuselnden,
Wellen, sanft kräuselnden,
Sonnenstrahl, eilender,
Nirgend verweilender:
Die mir mit Schmerze, ach!
Dies treue Herze brach –
Grüsst von dem Fliehenden
Welt hinaus ziehenden,
Welt hinaus ziehenden!

6. Far Away

Woe to those fleeing,
through the world wandering
Strange places travelling,
no home remembering
Birth place abandoning,
friendships relinquishing
No blessings follow,
oh as on their way they go,
as on their way they go.

Heart filled with yearning,
Tears always burning
Endless longing
for homeland calling
Heart that is sighing,
hope that is dying
Evening stars twinkling,
hopelessly sinking,
hopelessly sinking.

Breezes are rustling,
streams softly rippling,
Sunbeams are hurrying,
nowhere are tarrying
She who such love awoke,
Ah, then my true heart broke
Bring to her greeting
from one still fleeing,
from the world fleeing.

Breezes are rustling,
streams softly rippling,
Sunbeams are hurrying,
nowhere are tarrying
She who such love awoke,
Ah, then my true heart broke
Bring to her greetings
from one still fleeing,
from the world fleeing.

7. Abschied

Ade, Du muntre, Du fröhliche Stadt, Ade!
Schon scharret mein Rösslein mit lustigem Fuss;
Jetzt nimm noch den letzten, den scheidenden Gruss.
Du hast mich wohl niemals noch traurig gesehn,
So kann es auch jetzt nicht beim Abschied geschehn,
So kann es auch jetzt nicht beim Abschied geschehn
Ade, Du muntre, Du fröhliche Stadt, Ade!

Ade, Ihr Bäume, Ihr Gärten so grün, Ade!
Nun reit' ich am silbernen Strome entlang,
Weit schallend ertönet mein Abschiedsgesang,
Nie habt Ihr ein trauriges Lied gehört,
So wird Euch auch keines beim Scheiden beschert,
So wird Euch auch keines beim Scheiden beschert
Ade, Ihr Bäume, Ihr Gärten so grün, Ade!

Ade, Ihr freundlichen Mägdlein dort, Ade!
Was schaut Ihr aus blumenumduftetem Haus
Mit schelmischen, lockenden Blicken heraus?
Wie sonst, so grüss' ich und schaue mich um,
Doch nimmer wend' ich mein Rösslein um,
Doch nimmer wend' ich mein Rösslein um.

7. Farewell

Farewell you happy and lively town, farewell
Already my pony is stamping the ground
So take your last leave, let your blessings resound
It's true you have not seen me sad nor yet will
As from you I part and repeat my farewell
As from you I part and repeat my farewell
Farewell you happy and lively town, farewell.

Farewell you trees and you gardens so green, farewell
I ride down the path by the silvery stream
My parting song rings far and wide to proclaim
That never a sad song from my lips would flow
And likewise, gaily I'll sing as I go,
And likewise, gaily I'll sing as I go
Farewell you trees and you gardens so green, farewell.

Farewell you friendly young maidens there, farewell
You gaze through the windows of flower scented rooms
With impish looks to entice me back home
I hail you as always and glance round, of course
But never will I turn back my horse,
But never will I turn back my horse

Ade, Ihr freundlichen Mägdlein dort, Ade!	Farewell you friendly young maidens there, farewell.
Ade, liebe Sonne, so gehst Du zur Ruh', Ade!	Farewell dearest sun, as you go to your rest, farewell
Nun schimmert der blinkenden Sterne Gold.	Now twinkle the glimmering stars of gold
Wie bin ich Euch Sternlein am Himmel so hold,	How clear in the sky and so dear to behold
Durchziehn wir die Welt auch weit und breit,	We travel the world so far and wide
Ihr gebt überall uns das treue Geleit,	And you shine everywhere as a true faithful guide,
Ihr gebt überall uns das treue Geleit.	And you shine everywhere as a true faithful guide
Ade, liebe Sonne, so gehst Du zur Ruh', Ade!	Farewell dearest sun as you go to your rest, farewell.
Ade, Du schimmerndes Fensterlein hell, Ade!	Farewell you windows that shimmer with light, farewell
Du glänzest so traulich mit dämmerndem Schein	Your gleam is so friendly as darkness has grown
Und ladest so freundlich ins Hüttchen uns ein.	And kindly invites us to enter your home
Vorüber, ach, ritt ich so manches mal	So after I rode here, ah many a time
Und wär' es denn heute zum letzten mal?	Can this be the day for the final time?
Und wär' es denn heute zum letzten mal?	Can this be the day for the final time?
Ade, Du schimmerndes Fensterlein hell, Ade!	Farewell you windows that shimmer with light, farewell.
Ade, Ihr Sterne, verhüllet Euch grau! Ade!	Farewell you stars, put on your grey veil, farewell
Des Fensterlein trübes, verschimmerndes Licht	One sad little window with shimmering light
Ersetzt Ihr unzähligen Sterne mir nicht;	Could not be replaced by all the stars of the night
Darf ich hier nicht weilen, muss hier vorbei,	I can never stay here but must pass by
Was hilft es, folgt Ihr mir noch so treu!	What help to me is your path on high

Darf ich hier nicht weilen, muss hier vorbei,
Was hilft es, folgt Ihr mir noch so treu!
Ade, Ihr Sterne, verhüllet Euch grau!
  Ade!

I can never stay here but must pass by
What help to me is your path on high
Farewell you stars put on your grey veil,
  farewell.

8. Der Atlas

Ich unglücksel'ger Atlas,
Ich unglücksel'ger Atlas! eine Welt,
Die ganze Welt der Schmerzen muss ich tragen,
Die ganze Welt, muss ich tragen.
Ich trage Unerträgliches,
Und brechen will mir das Herz im Leibe.

Du stolzes Herz, du hast es ja gewollt!
Du wolltest glücklich sein, unendlich glücklich,
Oder unendlich elend, Oder unendlich elend,
Stolzes Herz, Und jetzo bist du elend.

Ich unglücksel'ger Atlas,
Ich unglücksel'ger Atlas!
Die ganze Welt der Schmerzen muss ich tragen,
Die ganze Welt, muss ich tragen.
Die ganze Welt der Schmerzen muss ich tragen,

8. Atlas

I am unhappy Atlas,
I am unhappy Atlas, This great world,
The whole great world of sorrow is my burden,
This whole great world is my burden.
I bear the most unbearable,
My heart is breaking within my body.

You boastful heart, you brought it on yourself
You wanted endless joy, unending joy
Or endless sorrow, unending sorrow
Boastful heart, you're left with only sorrow.

I am unhappy Atlas,
I am unhappy Atlas,
This whole great world of sorrow is my burden
The whole great world is my burden
This whole great world of sorrow is my burden.

9. Ihr Bild

Ich stand in dunkeln Träumen,
Und starrt' ihr Bildnis an,
Und das geliebte Antlitz
Heimlich zu leben begann.

Um ihre Lippen zog sich
Ein Lächeln wunderbar,
Und wie von Wehmutstränen
Erglänzte ihr Augenpaar.

Auch meine Tränen flossen
Mir von den Wangen herab
Und ach, ich kann es nicht glauben,
Dass ich dich verloren hab'!

9. Your Portrait

I stand before her portrait
With thoughts I can't explain
And those beloved features
Seemed to be living again

A smile of wondrous beauty
All round her lips did rise
And then the saddest teardrops
Were lit by the gleam in her eyes

Then my own tears were falling
And down my own cheeks did flow
And ah, I cannot believe it
How I lost you, I'll never know.

10. Das Fischermädchen

Du schönes Fischermädchen,
Treibe den Kahn ans Land;
Komm zu mir und setze dich nieder,
Wir kosen Hand in Hand.
Komm zu mir und setze dich nieder,
Wir kosen Hand in Hand,
Wir kosen Hand in Hand.

Leg an mein Herz dein Köpfchen,
Und fürchte dich nicht zu sehr;
Vertraust du dich doch sorglos
Täglich dem wilden Meer,
Vertraust du dich doch sorglos
Täglich dem wilden Meer,
Täglich dem wilden Meer.

Mein Herz gleicht ganz dem Meere,
Hat Sturm und Ebb' und Flut,
Und manche schöne Perle
In seiner Tiefe ruht,
Und manche schöne Perle
In seiner Tiefe ruht,
In seiner Tiefe ruht.

10. The Fisher Girl

You lovely fisher maiden
Bring in your boat to land
Come to me and sit beside me
Entwining hand in hand.
Come to me and sit beside me
Entwining hand in hand,
Entwining hand in hand

Lay on my heart your dear head
And do not mistrust me so
Each day you sail so carefree
Where raging tempest blow.
Each day you sail so carefree
Where raging tempest blow,
Where raging tempest blow.

My heart's just like the ocean
Where storm and tides are made
And many lovely pearls lie
Within its deepest bed,
And many lovely pearls lie
Within its deepest bed,
Within its deepest bed.

11. Die Stadt

Am fernen Horizonte
Erscheint, wie ein Nebelbild,
Die Stadt mit ihren Türmen
In Abenddämmrung gehüllt.

Ein feuchter Windzug kräuselt
Die graue Wasserbahn;
Mit traurigem Takte rudert
Der Schiffer in meinem Kahn.

Die Sonne hebt sich noch einmal
Leuchtend vom Boden empor,
Und zeigt mir jene Stelle,
Wo ich das Liebste verlor.

11. The Town

The distant far horizon
Appears in a misty cloud
A town with lofty steeples
Is veiled in twilight's grey shroud.

The moisture laden breezes
Across grey water ride
With solemn and measured rowing
The oarsman, my boat will guide.

The sun is once more arising
Shining on earth from above
And shows to me that township
Where I have lost my dear love.

12. Am Meer

Das Meer erglänzte weit hinaus
Im letzten Abendscheine;
Wir sassen am einsamen Fischerhaus,
Wir sassen stumm und alleine.

Der Nebel stieg, das Wasser schwoll,
Die Möwe flog hin und wieder;
Aus deinen Augen liebevoll
Fielen die Tränen nieder.

Ich sah sie fallen auf deine
    Hand,
Und bin aufs Knie gesunken;
Ich hab' von deiner weissen Hand
Die Tränen fortgetrunken.

Seit jener Stunde verzehrt sich mein
    Leib,
Die Seele stirbt vor Sehnen;
Mich hat das unglücksel'ge Weib
Vergiftet mit ihren Tränen.

12. By the Sea

The sea was glinting far and wide
In evening's fading twilight
A fisherman's hut we sat beside
Alone we sat there and silent.

The mist rolled in, the ocean swelled
The sea birds above us calling
And then your loving eyes were filled
Tears down your cheeks were falling.

I watched them dropping upon your
    hand
Then on my knees I was sinking
And from your white and gentle hand
Your teardrops I was drinking.

That fatal moment is within me
    still
My soul had died from yearning
I'm poisoned by that saddened girl
The tears that I drank are still burning.

13. Der Doppelgänger

Still ist die Nacht, es ruhen die Gassen,
In diesem Hause wohnte mein Schatz;
Sie hat schon längst die Stadt verlassen,
Doch steht noch das Haus auf demselben Platz.

Da steht auch ein Mensch und starrt in die Höhe,
Und ringt die Hände, vor Schmerzens Gewalt;
Mir graust es, wenn ich sein Antlitz sehe –
Der Mond zeigt mir meine eigne Gestalt.

Du Doppelgänger! du bleicher Geselle!
Was äffst du nach mein Liebesleid,
Das mich gequält auf dieser Stelle,
So manche Nacht, in alter Zeit?

13. The Double

Still is the night, the streets are asleep now
Here lived my sweetheart in this same house
She left the town so long ago now
Yet still stands the house in the same place.

And then from the house a man stands there staring
He wrings his hands in grief stricken loss
I shudder at the form I see appearing
The moon reveals my own face in the glass.

You pale reflection, you ghostly companion
Why mock the love I suffer so
With all the pain this place has given
So many nights so long ago.

14. Die Taubenpost

Ich hab' eine Brieftaub in meinem Sold,
Die ist gar ergeben und treu,
Sie nimmt mir nie das Ziel zu kurz,
Und fliegt auch nie vorbei.

Ich sende sie vieltausendmal
Auf Kundschaft täglich hinaus,
Vorbei an manchem lieben Ort,
Bis zu der Liebsten Haus,
Bis zu der Liebsten Haus.

Dort schaut sie zum Fenster heimlich
    hinein,
Belauscht ihren Blick und Schritt,
Gibt meine Grüsse scherzend ab
Und nimmt die ihren mit.

Kein Briefchen brauch' ich zu schreiben
    mehr,
Die Träne selbst geb' ich ihr:
O sie verträgt sie sicher nicht,
Gar eifrig dient sie mir,
Gar eifrig dient sie mir.

Bei Tag, bei Nacht, im Wachen, im
    Traum,
Ihr gilt das alles gleich:
Wenn sie nur wandern, wandern kann,
Dann ist sie überreich!

Sie wird nicht müd', sie wird nicht matt,
Der Weg ist stets ihr neu;
Sie braucht nicht Lockung, braucht
    nicht Lohn,
Die Taub' ist so mir treu,
Die Taub' ist so mir treu!

14. The Messenger

A messenger pigeon that I hold dear
Is ever devoted and loyal
She never flies too far from here
And always finds her goal.

I've sent her many thousand times
On daily missions she goes
Past many well-loved homes she flies
Straight to my darling's house,
Straight to my darling's house.

She peeps through the window, secretly
    she spies
And watches each step and glance
She gives my greeting to my love
And brings back hers at once.

No longer need I to write
    again
She carries my very tears
Oh yes, I know she'll guard them well
For me she truly serves,
For me she truly serves.

By day, by night, in dreams or
    awake
There never is complaint
When she can fly for flying's sake
Then she is well content.

She's never weary, she's never bored
Her way is always new
She needs no urging, nor no
    reward
She is to me so true,
She is to me so true.

Drum heg' ich sie auch so treu an der Brust,
Versichert des schönsten Gewinns;
Sie heisst, die Sehnsucht!
Kennt ihr sie?
Kennt ihr sie?
Die Botin treuen Sinn's,
Die Botin treuen Sinn's.

Drum heg' ich sie auch so treu an der Brust,
Versichert des schönsten Gewinns;
Sie heisst, die Sehnsucht!
Kennt ihr sie?
Kennt ihr sie?
Die Botin treuen Sinn's,
Die Botin treuen Sinn's.

Therefore to my heart I hold her so tight
Assured of her unending faith
Her name is longing,
did you know?
did you know?
The messenger of truth,
The messenger of truth.

Therefore to my heart I hold her so tight
Assured of her unending faith
Her name is longing,
did you know?
did you know?
The messenger of truth,
The messenger of truth.

Robert Schumann

Dichterliebe – A Poet's Love

Schumann's vocal masterpiece *Dichterliebe* (A Poet's Love), composed in the year of his marriage to Clara Wieck in 1840 to texts by the nineteenth century poet Heine has always been a vehicle for singers wishing to display their prowess on the art of singing and word communication.

Schumann's approach to song-writing was strongly coloured by the literary background of his youth, and equally important is the fact that he intended to become a pianist, not a composer.

His response to poetry made him more fastidious than some of his predecessors in the details of word-setting, especially in connection with repetition, and his love for the piano made him particularly eager to give it a generous share of musical material.

This is perhaps the reason why the cycle has always attracted pianists as well as singers.

Many of the songs have so much of the melody interpolated in the piano parts that they could, at the drop of a hat be transformed into lyrical Schumann-esque piano pieces.

The blending of the voice and piano parts is sheer genius, worthy of Schubert at his greatest.

In the first song 'How Lovely is the Month of May' Schumann doubles the voice and piano lines only in the first four bars then breaks away to new fields ever exploring the musical idiom in relation to the text.

The intimate interconnection of voice and piano can be seen in the way in which the piano is sometimes left to complete the vocal line. Sometimes the piano part alone suggests the mystery beneath the poem's surface, and the only time we meet with a repeated chord in the accompaniment comes in the song 'I Bear No Grudge'.

Of all the beautiful songs contained in the cycle I would personally place 'Alone on a Summer Morning' among the greatest miniatures in the whole of music.

Schumann's rich sentiment and Heine's biting terseness act as correctives to each other providing a balance between voice and piano which is perfectly maintained throughout the sixteen songs.

After the bitterness of the final song the extended piano postlude with its beautiful slowly rippling arpeggios, makes an overwhelming, haunting effect.

Had he composed no other songs future generations can hardly fail to count him among the greatest of German song-writers.

© Philip Rodden

1. Im wunderschönen Monat Mai

Im wunderschönen Monat Mai,
Als alle Knospen sprangen,
Da ist in meinem Herzen
Die Liebe aufgegangen.

Im wunderschönen Monat Mai,
Als alle Vögel sangen,
Da hab' ich ihr gestanden
Mein Sehnen und Verlangen.

1. How Lovely is the Month of May

How lovely is the month of May
when all the buds are bursting,
within my heart is rising
the love of which I'm thirsting.

How lovely is the month of May,
when all the birds are singing,
I told my love the secret
of my desire and longing.

2. Aus meinen Tränen sprießen

Aus meinen Tränen spriessen
Viel blühende Blumen hervor,
Und meine Seufzer werden
Ein Nachtigallenchor.

Und wenn du mich lieb hast, Kindchen,
Schenk' ich dir die Blumen all',
Und vor deinem Fenster soll klingen
Das Lied der Nachtigall.

2. Where'er my Tears are Falling

Where'er my tears are falling
the flowers of my love will soon throng,
and in my sighing rises
a Nightingale's sweet song.

And if my dear child you love me,
all the flowers to you I'll bring,
and before your window in chorus
the Nightingale shall sing.

3. Die Rose, die Lilie, die Taube, die Sonne

Die Rose, die Lilie, die Taube, die Sonne,
Die liebt' ich einst alle in Liebeswonne.
Ich lieb' sie nicht mehr, ich liebe
 alleine die Kleine, die Feine,
 die Reine, die Eine;
Sie selber, aller Liebe Wonne,
Ist Rose und Lilie
 und Taube und Sonne.
ich liebe alleine, die Kleine,
 die Feine, die Reine,
 die Eine, die Eine.

3. The Rose and the Lily

The rose and the lily, the dove and the sun,
once I loved with my heart, yes I loved every one.
I love them no more, I give all my love
 to the dearest, the fairest,
 the purist, the only one.
She is my own delightful love,
she's my rose and my lily,
 my sun and my dove.
Yes, I give all my love to the dearest
 the fairest, the purist,
 the only one, the only one.

4. Wenn ich in deine Augen seh

Wenn ich in deine Augen seh',
So schwindet all' mein Leid und Weh';
Doch wenn ich küsse deinen Mund,
So werd' ich ganz und gar gesund.

Wenn ich mich lehn' an deine Brust,
Kommt's über mich wie Himmelslust;
Doch wenn du sprichst: ich liebe dich!
So muss ich weinen bitterlich.

4. I Gaze into your Tender Eyes

I look once more into your eyes
and all my pain and sorrow flies;
and when I kiss those lips adored,
my very being is restored.

When I recline upon your breast,
comes all delight and heavenly rest;
But when you say: 'I love thee',
then I must weep most bitterly.

5. Ich will meine Seele tauchen

Ich will meine Seele tauchen
In den Kelch der Lilie hinein;
Die Lilie soll klingend hauchen
Ein Lied von der Liebsten mein.

Das Lied soll schauern und beben,
Wie der Kuss von ihrem Mund,
Den sie mir einst gegeben
In wunderbar süsser Stund'.

5. I Plunge my Soul in the Lily's Petals

I'll plunge my soul deeply
in the lily's petals divine;
The lily shall echo my sighing,
the song of this love of mine.

That song shall flutter and quiver,
like the trembling of her kiss.
The kiss that she once gave me
in wonderful, sweetest bliss.

6. Im Rhein, im heiligen Strome

Im Rhein, im heiligen Strome,
Da spiegelt sich in den Well'n
Mit seinem grossen Dome,
Das grosse, heilige Köln.

Im Dom da steht ein Bildnis,
Auf gold'nem Leder gemalt;
In meines Lebens Wildnis
Hat's freundlich hineingestrahlt.

Es schweben Blumen und Eng'lein
Um unsre liebe Frau;
Die Augen, die Lippen, die Wäng'lein,
Die gleichen der Liebsten genau.

6. The Rhine's Holy River

The Rhine most sacred of rivers,
reflects the shimmering stone.
That vast and spired cathedral,
that great and holy Cologne.

Inside there stands a portrait
on golden leather so bright;
Which on my life's own wilderness
sheds kindliest rays of light.

Above our lady angels hover and
round her flowers grow;
The eyes soft reflection, the lips and complexion,
reminds me of the one I used to know.

7. Ich grolle nicht

Ich grolle nicht, und wenn das Herz auch bricht,
Ewig verlor'nes Lieb, ewig verlor'nes Lieb!
ich grolle nich, ich grolle nicht.
Wie du auch strahlst in Diamantenpracht,
Es fällt kein Strahl in deines Herzens Nacht.
Das weiss ich längst.

Ich grolle nicht, und wenn das Herz auch bricht,
Ich sah dich ja im Traume,
Und sah die Nacht in deines Herzens Raume,
Und sah die Schlang', die dir am Herzen frisst,
Ich sah, mein Lieb, wie sehr du elend bist.
Ich grolle nicht, Ich grolle nicht.

7. I Bear No Grudge

No grudge I bear although my heart must break.
For ever lost is love, for ever lost is love,
I bear no grudge, I bear no grudge.
I saw you shine in diamonds splendour bright,
Yet not one ray falls in your heart's dark night.
I've known it long.

No grudge I bear although my heart must break.
In dreams when I am sleeping
I see the night that in your soul is creeping.
I see the serpent feeding on your heart,
I see my love how wretched now you are.
No grudge I bear within my heart.

8. Und wüßten's die Blumen, die kleinen

Und wüssten's die Blumen, die kleinen,
Wie tief verwundet mein Herz,
Sie würden mit mir weinen,
Zu heilen meinen Schmerz.

Und wüssten's die Nachtigallen,
Wie ich so traurig und krank,
Sie liessen fröhlich erschallen
Erquickenden Gesang.

Und wüssten sie mein Wehe,
Die goldenen Sternelein,
Sie kämen aus ihrer Höhe,
Und sprächen Trost mir ein.

Sie alle können's nicht wissen,
Nur eine kennt meinen Schmerz:
Sie hat ja selbst zerrissen,
Zerrissen mir das Herz.

8. If Only the Tiniest Flowers

If only the tiniest flowers
could know my pain and my grief,
I'm sure they would weep with me
to help me find relief.

If nightingales also knew it,
how sick I am and how sad,
they would relieve all my sorrow
with songs to make me glad.

And If they knew my sadness,
the bright little golden stars
would come down to me from heaven
with words to end my cares.

But none of them know my sorrow,
one only has played her part,
for she indeed has broken,
has broken my poor heart.

9. Das ist ein Flöten und Geigen

Das ist ein Flöten und Geigen,
Trompeten schmettern darein,
Trompeten schmettern darein;
Da tanzt wohl den Hochzeitsreigen
Die Herzallerliebste mein,
die Herzallerliebste mein.

Das ist ein Klingen und Dröhnen,
das ist ein Klingen und Dröhnen,
Ein Pauken und ein Schalmei'n;
Dazwischen schluchzen und stöhnen,
dazwischen schluchzen und stöhnen
die lieblichen Engelein.

9. The Flutes and Fiddles are Playing

The flutes and fiddles are playing,
the trumpets flourish and bray,
the trumpets flourish and bray.
The girl that I loved is dancing,
is this then her wedding day?
is this then her wedding day?

With all the piping and droning,
With all the piping and droning,
and drumming that fills the air.
I hear the sobbing and groaning,
I hear the sobbing and groaning
of angels in dark despair.

10. Hör' ich das Liedchen klingen

Hör' ich das Liedchen klingen,
Das einst die Liebste sang,
So will mir die Brust zerspringen
Von wildem Schmerzendrang.

Es treibt mich ein dunkles Sehnen
Hinauf zur Waldeshöh',
Dort löst sich auf in Tränen
Mein übergrosses Weh'.

10. If Little Songs Remind Me

If little songs remind me
of those she used to sing,
with anguish my heart is breaking
wild thoughts and grief they bring.

And driven by darkest longing
to hillside woods I climb,
and there dissolves in weeping
this deepest grief of mine.

11. Ein Jüngling liebt ein Mädchen

Ein Jüngling liebt ein Mädchen,
Die hat einen andern erwählt;
Der andre liebt eine andre,
Und hat sich mit dieser vermählt.

Das Mädchen nimmt aus Ärger
Den ersten besten Mann,
Der ihr in den Weg gelaufen;
Der Jüngling ist übel dran.

Es ist eine alte Geschichte,
Doch bleibt sie immer neu;
Und wem sie just passieret,
Dem bricht das Herz entzwei.

11. A Boy Once Loved a Maiden

A boy once loved a maiden,
she sighed for another instead,
but he in turn loved another
and soon he was happily wed.

The maiden felt rejected
and without care or heed,
she wed the next man to woo her,
the first boy was hurt indeed.

It is a familiar story
but stays for ever new
and every time it happens
it breaks a heart in two.

12. Am leuchtenden Sommermorgen

Am leuchtenden Sommermorgen
Geh' ich im Garten herum.
Es flüstern und sprechen die Blumen,
Ich aber wandle stumm.

Es flüstern und sprechen die Blumen,
Und schau'n mitleidig mich an:
"Sei unsrer Schwester nicht böse,
Du trauriger, blasser Mann."

12. Alone on a Summer Morning

Alone on a summer morning,
sadly the garden I roam.
Around me the flowers are whispering,
I walk in silence on.

The flowers are still whispering together
they know how wretched I am.
"Please bear our sister no malice
you pale and so sorrowful man".

13. Ich hab' im Traum geweinet

Ich hab' im Traum geweinet,
Mir träumte, du lägest im Grab.
Ich wachte auf, und die Träne
Floss noch von der Wange herab.

Ich hab' im Traum geweinet,
Mir träumt', du verliessest mich.
Ich wachte auf, und ich weinte
Noch lange bitterlich.

Ich hab' im Traum geweinet,
Mir träumte, du wär'st mir noch gut.
Ich wachte auf, und noch immer
Strömt meine Tränenflut.

13. I Wept as I Lay Dreaming

I wept as I was dreaming,
a grave was your resting place.
Then I awoke, and a tear drop
rolled down my trembling face.

I wept as I was dreaming
I dreamt you were gone from me,
Then I awoke, and remembering,
wept long and bitterly.

I wept as I was dreaming,
I dreamt that your heart was still true.
Then I awoke, and the teardrops
flowed from my eyes anew.

14. Allnächtlich im Traume

Allnächtlich im Traume seh' ich dich
Und sehe dich freundlich grüssen,
Und laut aufweinend stürz' ich mich
Zu deinen süssen Füssen.

Du siehest mich an wehmütiglich
Und schüttelst das blonde Köpfchen;
Aus deinen Augen schleichen sich
Die Perlentränentröpfchen.

Du sagst mir heimlich ein leises Wort
Und gibst mir den Strauss von Zypressen.
Ich wache auf, und der Strauss ist fort,
Und's Wort hab' ich vergessen.

14. Each Night-time I See You

Each night-time I see you in my dreams,
and there you are smiling, smiling kindly
and sobbing loudly through my tears
I fall before you blindly.

And sadly your eyes gaze into mine,
and shaking your head as if recalling,
and stealing slowly from your eyes
like pearls the tears are falling.

You whisper softly a secret word
and gave me the cypress wreath as a token.
Then I awake, and the wreath is gone,
the word I have forgotten.

15. Aus alten Märchen

Aus alten Märchen winkt es
Hervor mit weisser Hand,
Da singt es und da klingt es
Von einem Zauberland;

Wo bunte Blumen blühen
Im gold'nen Abendlicht,
Und lieblich duftend glühen,
Mit bräutlichem Gesicht;

Und grüne Bäume singen
Uralte Melodei'n,
Die Lüfte heimlich klingen,
Und Vögel schmettern drein;

Und Nebelbilder steigen
Wohl aus der Erd' hervor,
Und tanzen luft'gen Reigen
Im wunderlichen Chor;

Und blaue Funken brennen
An jedem Blatt und Reis,
Und rote Lichter rennen
Im irren, wirren Kreis;

Und laute Quellen brechen
Aus wildem Marmorstein.
Und seltsam in den Bächen
Strahlt fort der Widerschein.

Ach, ach, könnt' ich dorthin kommen,
Und dort mein Herz erfreu'n,
Und aller Qual entnommen,
Und frei und selig sein!

Ach! jenes Land der Wonne,
Das seh' ich oft im Traum,
Doch kommt die Morgensonne,
Zerfliesst's wie eitel Schaum,
Zerfliesst's wie eitel Schaum.

15. Old Fairy Tales

Old Fairy tales entice us to
come with beckoning hand.
There's singing and there's ringing
as from a magic land.

Where many flowers are blooming
in golden eventide,
and sweetly scented glow
like the face of every bride.

And green trees are singing
the tunes forgotten long,
and breezes softly murmur
to birds' melodious song.

And misty shapes appearing
are rising from the ground,
they dance in airy circles
in chorus round and round.

And sapphire sparks are burning
on every leaf and twig,
and bright red lights are
skipping a weird confusing jig.

Loud springs rush out from marble
and wildly rush downstream,
as strangely on those rivers
the weird reflections gleam.

Ah, ah, if I could only go there
to free my heart from pain,
so I could end my torment
and peace and joy regain.

I dream of that dear country,
a land to make my home,
but comes the morning sun,
dissolving dreams like foam,
dissolving dreams like foam.

16. Die alten, bösen Lieder

Die alten, bösen Lieder,
Die Träume bös' und arg,
Die lasst uns jetzt begraben,
Holt einen grossen Sarg.

Hinein leg' ich gar manches,
Doch sag' ich noch nicht was;
Der Sarg muss sein noch grösser,
Wie's Heidelberger Fass.

Und holt eine Totenbahre
Und Bretter fest und dick;
Auch muss sie sein noch länger,
Als wie zu Mainz die Brück'.

Und holt mir auch zwölf Riesen,
Die müssen noch stärker sein
Als wie der starke Christoph
Im Dom zu Köln am Rhein.

Die sollen den Sarg forttragen,
Und senken ins Meer hinab;
Denn solchem grossen Sarge
Gebührt ein grosses Grab.

Wisst ihr, warum der Sarg wohl
So gross und schwer mag sein?
Ich senkt' auch meine Liebe
Und meinen Schmerz hinein.

16. The Bad Old Songs are Gone

The bad old songs are gone now,
the painful dreams are past.
Its time they now were buried,
fetch me a coffin vast.

So much I lay inside it,
but what, I'll not say yet.
The coffin must be larger
than Heidelberg's great vat.

And fetch me a funeral carriage
with timbers thick and strong.
It must be even larger
than the bridge at Mainz is long.

And now I need twelve giants
the strongest of all their race,
as strong as Saint Christopher
in Cologne's most holy place.

The coffin they now shall carry
to plunge in the ocean's wave,
for such a mighty coffin
deserves a mighty grave.

So now you know the reason
the coffin was so vast.
I'm drowning all my love there,
so all my grief is past.

Robert Schumann

Liederkreis – Opus 24 (Heine)

At this time, Schumann is deeply in love.

"Dear Clara.
With thoughts of you I am brimming over with music. I will tell you all about it when next I see you".

And he wrote again,

"Dear Clara.
I am working very hard and sitting at the piano with thoughts of you at your loveliest".

To his publisher he wrote that the poetry of Heine added to his inspiration and devotion, and that he had worked long and joyfully.

1. Morgens steh' ich auf und frage

Morgens steh' ich auf und frage:
Kommt feins Liebchen heut?
Abends sink' ich hin und klage:
Ausblieb sie auch heut.

In der Nacht mit meinem Kummer
Lieg' ich schlaflos, lieg' ich wach;
Träumend, wie im halben Schlummer,
Träumend wandle ich bei Tag.

1. Every Morning I Wake Thinking

Every morning I wake thinking,
Will she come today?
Evening comes, my heart is sinking,
Once more she has stayed away.

All night long I lie in sorrow,
Sleepless in a dreamy haze,
And I'll walk around tomorrow,
Half asleep I pass the days.

2. Es treibt mich hin

Es treibt mich hin, es treibt mich her!
Noch wenige Stunden, dann soll ich sie
    schauen,
Sie selber, die schönste der schönen
    Jungfrauen;
Du armes Herz, was pochst du so
    schwer?

Die Stunden sind aber ein faules Volk!
Schleppen sich behaglich träge,
Schleichen gähnend ihre Wege;
Tummle dich, du faules Volk!

Tobende Eile mich treibend erfasst!
Aber wohl niemals liebten die Horen;
Niemals, niemals liebten die Horen
Heimlich im grausamen Bunde
    verschworen,
Spotten sich tückisch der Liebenden
    Hast.

2. I'm Rushing There

I'm rushing here, I'm rushing there,
It's just a few moments until our next
    meeting.
You poor fragile heart, how fast is your
    beating,
And she is the fairest of the
    fair.

The hours are such a lazy crowd,
Slowly moving in idle measure,
Creeping, yawning at their leisure,
Hurry on you lazy crowd.

Raging impatience seizes me fast,
But perhaps time has never known love,
Never, never known what is love,
Secretly, cruelly sworn not to
    move,
Mocking and spiteful they laugh at love's
    haste.

3. Ich wandelte unter den Bäumen

Ich wandelte unter den Bäumen
Mit meinem Gram allein;
Da kam das alte Träumen,
Und schlich mir ins Herz hinein.

Wer hat euch dies Wörtlein gelehret,
Ihr Vöglein in luftiger
  Höh'?
Schweigt still! wenn mein Herz es höret,
Dann tut es noch einmal so
  weh.

Es kam ein Jungfräulein
  gegangen,
Die sang es immerfort,
Da haben wir Vöglein
  gefangen
Das hübsche, goldne Wort.

Das sollt ihr mir nicht erzählen,
Ihr Vöglein wunderschlau;
Ihr wollt meinen Kummer mir stehlen,
Ich aber niemanden trau',
Ich aber niemanden trau'.

3. I Walk Under Leafy Branches

I walk under leafy branches
alone with all my pain;
Here came my distant fancies,
And stole through my heart again.

You birds flying round in the clearing,
Who taught you that little word you
  sing?
Oh hush, for my heart is hearing
Those words and the grief that they
  bring.

There came a young maiden here
  singing,
The same song we often heard,
That song through the woodland was
  ringing,
And those sweet golden words.

Don't tell me what I am feeling,
You birds so cruel and sly,
And why all my grief are you stealing?
On no one can I rely?
On no one can I rely?

4. Lieb' Liebchen

Lieb Liebchen, leg's Händchen aufs Herze mein;
Ach, hörst du, wie's pochet im Kämmerlein?
Da hauset ein Zimmermann schlimm und arg,
Der zimmert mir einen Totensarg.

Es hämmert und klopfet bei Tag und bei Nacht;
Es hat mich schon längst um den Schlaf gebracht.
Ach sputet Euch, Meister Zimmermann,
Damit ich balde schlafen kann.

4. Dear Love

Dear love lay your hand on this heart of mine;
And hear how it throbs in its room all the time,
Inside lives a carpenter, bad is he,
He's making a coffin – just for me.

By night and by day from the time he arrived;
He hammers and taps, of my sleep I'm deprived.
Oh then master carpenter work fast,
That I may soon sleep at last.

5. Schöne Wiege meiner Leiden

Schöne Wiege meiner Leiden,
Schönes Grabmal meiner Ruh',
Schöne Stadt, wir müssen scheiden,
Lebe wohl! ruf' ich dir zu,
Lebe wohl, lebe wohl!

Lebe wohl, du heil'ge Schwelle,
Wo da wandelt Liebchen traut;
Lebe wohl! du heil'ge Stelle,
Wo ich sie zuerst geschaut.
Lebe wohl, lebe wohl!

Hätt' ich dich doch nie gesehen,
Schöne Herzenskönigin!
Nimmer, nimmer wär es dann geschehen,
Dass ich jetzt so elend bin.

Nie wollt' ich dein Herze rühren,
Liebe hab' ich nie erfleht;
Nur ein stilles Leben führen
Wollt' ich, wo dein Odem weht,
Wo dein Odem weht.

Doch du drängst mich selbst von hinnen,
Bittre Worte spricht dein Mund;
Wahnsinn wühlt in meinen Sinnen,
Und mein Herz ist krank und wund.

Und die Glieder matt und träge
Schlepp' ich, schlepp' ich fort am Wanderstab,
Bis mein müdes Haupt ich lege
Ferne in ein kühles Grab.

Schöne Wiege meiner Leiden,
Schönes Grabmal meiner Ruh',
Schöne Stadt, wir müssen scheiden,,
Lebe wohl, lebe wohl!

5. Lovely Cradle of my Grieving

Lovely cradle of my grieving,
Lovely tomb where peace I knew,
Lovely town that I am leaving,
Farewell I call to you,
Farewell, farewell.

So farewell you sacred household,
Where my sweetheart passed her days;
And farewell you hallowed threshold,
Where she first returned my gaze.
Farewell, farewell.

Had your face I'd never seen,
Lovely queen of all my heart.
Never, never, this could not have been,
That I now so sad depart.

I knew not your heart was aching,
For your love I did not crave,
Just a peaceful life I'm seeking,
Breathing in the air you breathe,
Breathing in the air you breathe.

But you drove me into going,
Bitter words I'll hear no more;
Frenzied thoughts within me growing,
And my heart is sick and sore.

And with limbs so worn and feeble,
Dragging, dragging onward with my stave,
Till my weary head I cradle,
In a cool and distant silent grave.

Lovely cradle of my grieving,
Lovely tomb where peace I knew,
Lovely town that I am leaving,
Farewell, farewell.

6. Warte, warte wilder Schiffmann

Warte, warte, wilder Schiffmann,
Gleich folg' ich zum Hafen dir;
Gleich, gleich, gleich!
Von zwei Jungfrau nehm' ich Abschied,
Von Europa und von Ihr.

Blutquell, rinn' aus meinen Augen,
Blutquell, brich aus meinem Leib,
Dass ich mit dem heissen Blute
Meine Schmerzen niederschreib'.

Ei, mein Lieb, warum just heute
Schaudert dich, mein Blut zu sehn?
Sahst mich bleich und herzeblutend
Lange Jahre vor dir stehn! Oh!

Kennst du noch das alte Liedchen
Von der Schlang' im Paradies,
Die durch schlimme Apfelgabe
Unsern Ahn ins Elend stiess?

Alles Unheil brachten Äpfel!
Eva bracht' damit den Tod,
Eris brachte Trojas Flammen,
Du, du bracht'st beides, Flamm' und Tod.

6. Wait, Oh Wait Hasty Boatman

Wait, oh wait there hasty boatman,
Soon I'll follow to the harbour,
Soon, soon, soon.
From two loves I am departing,
From my country and from her.

Blood springs freely from my body,
Blood springs freely from my eyes,
Let me with the scalding blood flow,
Write the pain of my demise.

Ah, my love, why at this moment
Do you shake to see my blood?
You knew that my heart was bleeding,
All those years you understood! Oh!

Do you know the ancient story
How the snake in Paradise,
Gave to Eve the evil apple
Causing all of man's demise?

Evil started with this apple,
Eve, she brought us only death
Flames were brought to Troy by Paris,
You! you brought both the flames and death.

7. Berg und Burgen schaun herunter

Berg' und Burgen schaun herunter
In den spiegelhellen Rhein,
Und mein Schiffchen segelt munter,
Rings umglänzt von Sonnenschein,
Rings umglänzt von Sonnenschein.

Ruhig seh' ich zu dem Spiele
Goldner Wellen, kraus bewegt;
Still erwachen die Gefühle,
Die ich tief im Busen hegt',
Die ich tief im Busen hegt'.

Freundlich grüssend und verheissend
Lockt hinab des Stromes Pracht;
Doch ich kenn' ihn, oben gleissend,
Bringt sein Innres Tod und Nacht,
Bringt sein Innres Tod und Nacht.

Oben Lust, in Busen Tücken,
Strom, du bist der Liebsten Bild!
Die kann auch so freundlich nicken,
Lächelt auch so fromm und mild,
Lächelt auch so fromm und mild.

7. Hills and Castle Rise Prevailing

Hills and castle rise prevailing,
Mirrored is the river Rhine
Where my little boat is sailing
Where the suns rays brightly shine,
Where the suns rays brightly shine.

Silently I watch the breaking
Of the little golden waves;
Dreams I thought were dead are waking,
Rising from their silent graves,
Rising from their silent graves.

Splendid river bright and friendly
Lures me with its golden light;
Though its surface shines about me,
Down below dwells death and night,
Down below dwells death and night.

Outward joy but heart of malice,
My beloved and the Rhine,
She too lifts the friendly chalice
Smiles so gently, so divine,
Smiles so gently, so divine.

8. Anfangs wollt' ich fast verzagen

Anfangs wollt' ich fast verzagen,
Und ich glaubt', ich trüg' es nie;
Und ich hab' es doch getragen
Aber fragt mich nur nicht, wie?
Nicht, wie?

8. My Heart was Aching

At the start my heart was aching,
How could I have borne it so?
Now despair I am forsaking,
Only never ask me how,
Not how.

9. Mit Myrten und Rosen

Mit Myrthen und Rosen, lieblich und hold,
Mit duft'gen Cypressen und Flittergold,
Möcht' ich zieren dies Buch wie 'nen Totenschrein,
Und sargen meine Lieder hinein.

O könnt' ich die Liebe sargen hinzu!
Auf dem Grabe der Liebe wächst Blümlein der Ruh',
Da blüht es hervor, da pflückt man es ab,
Doch mir blüht's nur, wenn ich selber im Grab,
wenn ich selber im Grab.

Hier sind nun die Lieder, die einst so wild,
Wie ein Lavastrom, der dem Ätna entquillt,
Hervorgestürzt aus dem tiefsten Gemüt,
Und rings viel blitzende Funken versprüht!

Nun liegen sie stumm und totengleich,
Nun starren sie kalt und nebelbleich,
Doch aufs neu' die alte Glut sie belebt,
Wenn der Liebe Geist einst über sie schwebt,
Doch aufs neu' die alte Glut sie belebt,
Wenn der Liebe Geist einst über sie schwebt.

Und es wird mir im Herzen viel Ahnung laut;
Der Liebe Geist einst über sie taut;

9. With Myrtle and Roses

With myrtle and roses so fair to behold,
With fragrant cypress and leaf of gold,
I would like to adorn this book as a shrine,
And bury all these poems of mine.

If only my love could lie in that tomb,
On the grave of great love flowers of peace always bloom,
They grow there for you to pluck and to save,
But not for me till I lie in my grave,
Till I lie in my grave.

So here are my songs once so full of hope,
Flowing fast as lava on Mount Etna's slope,
They burst from the depths of my soul into light,
To shower the world with their radiance so bright.

They lie now so still in silent death,
As pale as the mist that covers the heath,
Yet the fire of old would quicken to flame,
If a loving spirit came once again,
Yet the fire of old would quicken to flame,
If a loving spirit came once again.

It was clear in my heart that I've known it long;
The ghost of love will breathe on my songs;

Einst kommt dies Buch in deine Hand, Du süsses Lieb, Du süsses Lieb im fernen Land.	Oh could you hold this book one day, My sweetest love, My sweetest love so far away.
Dann löst sich des Liedes Zauberbann, Die blassen Buchstaben schaun dich an, Sie schauen dir flehend ins schöne Aug', Und flüstern mit Wehmut und Liebeshauch.	Then gone is the spell that held them fast, The faded words will look up at last, And gaze with desire in your lovely eyes, And whisper with sadness of lovers' sighs.

Robert Schumann

Opus 35 (Kerner)

At the time of this cycle Schumann, as with all the great song composers, believed that fame and financial security might not come from song alone and that large works, opera and symphonies, would bring him, as a married man, the security and artistic fulfilment he needed.

The Kerner songs were composed at a time just before the strong desire to write symphonies had become so important, so it can be easily understood that these songs had a sense of overwhelming emotions, joy, sadness, loneliness, even madness.

There is certainly a darker element in these than in his earlier songs which might remind the listener of Schubert's *Winterreise*.

1. Lust der Sturmnacht

Wenn durch Berg und Tale draussen
Regen schauert, Stürme brausen,
Schild und Fenster hell erklirren,
Und in Nacht die Wandrer irren.

Ruht es sich so süss hier innen,
Aufgelöst in selges Minnen;
All der goldne Himmelsschimmer
Flieht herein ins stille Zimmer:

Reiches Leben, hab' Erbarmen!
Halt' mich fest in linden Armen!
Lenzesblumen aufwärts dringen,
Wölklein ziehn und Vöglein singen.

Ende nie, du Sturmnacht, wilde!
Klirrt, ihr Fenster, schwankt, ihr Schilde,
Bäumt euch, Wälder, braus', o Welle,
Mich umfängt des Himmels helle,
Mich umfängt des Himmels helle!

1. Joy in the Storm

Through the night when winds are roaring,
Storms are raging, rain is pouring,
Windows banging, inn signs creaking,
Folk, their gloomy way are seeking.

Then how sweet it is and peaceful
Lost within our love so blissful;
All the golden light of heaven
In our quiet room is given

Life abundant do not scold me,
In your gentle arms enfold me!
Until flowers are upwards springing,
Clouds float by and birds are singing.

Drive on storm, your rage displaying
Bang you windows, signs keep swaying,
Let the trees and waves be driven,
I'm embraced by radiant heaven,
I'm embraced by radiant heaven.

2. Stirb', Lieb' und Freud'!

Zu Augsburg steht ein hohes Haus,
Nah' bei dem alten Dom,
Da tritt am hellen Morgen aus
Ein Mägdelein gar fromm;
Gesang erschallt,
Zum Dome wallt
Die liebe, die liebe Gestalt.

Dort vor Maria's heilig' Bild
Sie betend niederkniet,
Der Himmel hat ihr Herz erfüllt,
Und alle Weltlust flieht:
O Jungfrau rein!
Lass mich allein
Dein eigen sein!"

Alsbald der Glocken dumpfer Klang
Die Betenden erweckt,
Das Mägdlein wallt die Hall' entlang,
Es weiss nicht, was es trägt;
Am Haupte ganz,
Von Himmelsglanz,
Einen Lilienkranz.

Mit Staunen schauen all' die Leut'
Dies Kränzlein licht im Haar.
Das Mägdlein aber wallt nicht weit,
Tritt vor den Hochaltar:
Zur Nonne weiht
Mich arme Maid!
Stirb', Lieb' und Freud'!"

2. Death to Love and Joy

In Augsburg stands a most imposing house,
With an old cathedral close by,
And one bright morning from that house
Stepped a maiden pure and shy.
While hymns they play,
She makes her way,
The dear one, the dear one to pray.

There under Mary's holy gaze,
She bends her knee in praise.
The heavens from now her heart will own,
And all worldly joys have flown.
Oh, virgin fine,
Give me a sign,
Let me be thine

When soon the muffled bells rang out
The congregation rose from prayer,
Along the nave she seemed to float
She knew not what she wore in her hair;
A wreath so bright,
Of lilies white,
Lit by heavenly light.

The people there were all amazed
At the wreath shining in her hair.
The maiden stopped, her eyes were raised,
As she knelt before the high alter.
Oh holy one,
Make me a nun!
Let joy be gone.

Gott, gib, dass dieses Mägdelein Ihr Kränzlein friedlich trag', Es ist die Herzallerliebste mein, Bleibt's bis zum jüngsten Tag. Sie weiss es nicht, Mein Herz zerbricht, Stirb', Lieb' und Licht!	God grant that this sweet maiden May find her heart's desire, She is my heart's own beloved one Till judgement day is here. She knows it not, It breaks my heart, Die, love and light!

3. Wanderlied

Wohlauf, noch getrunken Den funkelnden Wein!
Ade nun, ihr Lieben! Geschieden muss sein.
Ade nun, ihr Berge, Du väterlich Haus!
Es treibt in die Ferne Mich mächtig hinaus.

Die Sonne, sie bleibet Am Himmel nicht stehn,
Es treibt sie, durch Länder Und Meere zu gehn.
Die Woge nicht haftet Am einsamen Strand,
Die Stürme, sie brausen Mit Macht durch das Land.

Mit eilenden Wolken Der Vogel dort zieht,
Und singt in der Ferne Ein heimatlich Lied.
So treibt es den Burschen Durch Wälder und Feld,
Zu gleichen der Mutter, Der wandernden Welt.

Da grüssen ihn Vögel Bekannt überm Meer,
Sie flogen von Fluren Der Heimat hieher;
Da duften die Blumen Vertraulich um ihn,
Sie trieben vom Lande Die Lüfte dahin.

3. Song of the Wanderer

Come on, one more glass of the sparkling wine!
Let's drink my dear friends, to this parting of mine.
Farewell now you mountains and homelands I know,
I'm stirred by a force that compels me to go.

The sun is not still in the heavens on high,
It sees land and oceans while riding the sky.
The waves do not cling to the lonely strand,
The storms rage and bluster all over the land.

The birds fly above where clouds float along,
In lands far away, they will sing their native song.
The young man is driven to roam thro woods and field,
And like Mother Nature, must wander the world.

He's greeted by birds over seas they have flown,
They flew from the woodlands and meadows of home
The fragrance around him of flowers and trees,
Are borne from his homeland on a warm summer breeze.

Die Vögel, die kennen Sein väterlich Haus,	The birds all remember the land of his birth,
Die Blumen, die pflanzt' er Der Liebe zum Strauss,	The flowers that made garlands he sowed in the earth.
Und Liebe, die folgt ihm, Sie geht ihm zur Hand,	And loves now surrounds him to be close at hand,
So wird ihm zur Heimat Das ferneste Land,	So he feels at home in the most distant land,
So wird ihm zur Heimat Das ferneste Land.	So he feels at home in the most distant land.
Wohlauf, noch getrunken Den funkelnden Wein!	Come on, one more glass of the sparkling wine!
Ade nun, ihr Lieben! Geschieden muss sein.	Let's drink my dear friends, to this parting of mine.
Ade nun, ihr Berge, Du väterlich Haus!	Farewell now you mountains and homelands I know,
Es treibt in die Ferne Mich mächtig hinaus,	I'm stirred by a force that compels me to go,
Es treibt in die Ferne Mich mächtig hinaus.	I'm stirred by a force that compels me to go.

4. Erstes Grün

Du junges Grün, du frisches Gras!
Wie manches Herz durch dich genas,
Das von des Winters Schnee erkrankt,
O wie mein Herz nach dir verlangt!

Schon wächst du aus der Erde Nacht,
Wie dir mein Aug' entgegen lacht!
Hier in des Waldes stillem Grund
Drück ich dich, Grün, an Herz und Mund.

Wie treibt's mich von den Menschen fort!
Mein Leid das hebt kein Menschenwort,
Nur junges Grün, ans Herz gelegt
Macht, dass mein Herze stiller schlägt.

4. First Green

You grass so new, you fresh green field,
How many hearts by you were healed,
That languished all the winter through,
Oh how my heart has longed for you.

You grow so strong from darkened earth,
And how my eyes light up with mirth.
Here in the woodlands quietness
My heart and lips to you I press.

In fellow men I've no belief,
No words they say can end my grief.
My beating heart is calmer made
When on my heart your green is laid.

5. Sehnsucht nach der Waldgegend

Wär' ich nie aus euch gegangen,
Wälder, hehr und wunderbar!
Hieltet liebend mich umfangen
Doch so lange, lange Jahr!

Wo in euren Dämmerungen
Vogelsang und Silberquell,
Ist auch manches Lied entsprungen
Meinem Busen, frisch und hell.

Euer Wogen, euer Hallen,
Euer Säuseln nimmer müd',
Eure Melodien alle
Weckten in der Brust das Lied.

Hier in diesen weiten Triften
Ist mir alles öd' und stumm,
Und ich schau in blauen Lüften
Mich nach Wolkenbildern um.

Wenn ihr's in den Busen zwinget,
Regt sich selten nur das Lied:
Wie der Vogel halb nur singet,
Den von Baum und Blatt man schied.

5. Longing for the Forest

Would that you had tried to hold me,
Sacred woodland I hold so dear.
With your love you did enfold me
Though so long, so long the year.

In your twilight birds were singing
Where the silver streamlets play,
From my heart the songs were springing,
Songs of love so fresh and gay.

Rivers surging echoes sounding,
All your rustling never did rest,
All your melodies surrounding
Woke the songs within my breast.

Here across this empty pasture
All is desolate and dry,
And I gaze above to capture
Pictures in the clouds on high.

Though you force my heart to waken,
Songs will seldom stir my heart.
As a bird's song is forsaken
When from leaf and tree it parts.

6. Auf das Trinkglas eines verstorbenen Freundes

Du herrlich Glas, nun stehst du leer,
Glas, das er oft mit Lust gehoben;
Die Spinne hat rings um dich her
Indes den düstren Flor gewoben.

Jetzt sollst du mir gefüllet sein
Mondhell mit Gold der deutschen
   Reben!
In deiner Tiefe heil'gen Schein
Schau ich hinab mit frommem Beben.

Was ich erschau' in deinem Grund
Ist nicht Gewöhnlichen zu
   nennen.
Doch wird mir klar zu dieser Stund',
Wie nichts den Freund vom Freund
   kann trennen.

Auf diesen Glauben, Glas so hold!
Trink' ich dich aus mit hohem Mute.
Klar spiegelt sich der Sterne Gold,
Pokal, in deinem teuren Blute!

Still geht der Mond das Tal entlang.
Ernst tönt die mitternächtge Stunde.
Leer steht das Glas! Der heilge Klang
Tönt nach in dem kristall'nen Grunde.

6. To the Glass From Which a Dead Friend Drank

You noble glass, now there you stand,
Glass that he often raised to living.
The spider spins a silken strand
To weave his solemn veil of grieving.

Now once again be filled and raised
With moonbright gold of Rheinland
   wines.
When in your sacred depths I gaze
I tremble for our bygone times.

When I look deep into your heart
Few men could know such
   understanding.
It's clear to me now from the start,
How friendship true is never
   ending.

In this belief O blessed glass,
Let me now drink with heart uplifted.
Your cherished blood my lips caress,
The golden stars in you reflected.

Silent the moon moves down the vale.
Gravely the midnight bell is sounding.
Drained stands the glass, the holy bell
All round its crystal bowl is resounding.

7. Wanderung

Wohlauf und frisch gewandert
Ins unbekannte Land!
Zerrissen, ach zerrissen,
Ist manches teure Band.

Ihr heimatlichen Kreuze,
Wo ich oft betend lag,
Ihr Bäume, ach, ihr Hügel,
O blickt mir segnend nach.

Noch schläft die weite Erde,
Kein Vogel weckt den Hain,
Doch bin ich nicht verlassen,
Doch bin ich nicht allein,

Denn, ach, auf meinem Herzen
Trag' ich ihr teures Pfand,
Ich fühl's, und Erd und Himmel
Sind innig mir verwandt,
Sind innig mir verwandt.

7. Walking

I'm off to briskly wander
To lands that are unknown.
I've broken, yes I've broken,
My ties with all at home

You shrines across my homeland,
Where I would kneel and pray,
You forests, ah, you hillsides,
Oh bless me on my way.

And while the world is sleeping,
Before birds sing at dawn,
I'll know I'm not forsaken,
I'll know I'm not alone.

For in my heart I carry
Her cherished pledge of love,
I feel it and I'm closer
To earth and heaven above,
To earth and heaven above.

8. Stille Liebe

Könnt' ich dich in Liedern preisen,
Säng' ich dir das längste Lied.
Ja, ich würd' in allen Weisen,
Dich zu singen nimmer müd'!

Doch was immer mich betrübte,
Ist, dass ich nur immer stumm,
Tragen kann dich, Herzgeliebte,
In des Busens Heiligtum.

Dieser Schmerz hat mich bezwungen,
Dass ich sang dies kleine Lied,
Doch von bitterm Leid durchdrungen,
Dass noch kein's auf dich geriet.

8. Silent Love

If I could but sing your praises,
Every love song you would hear.
yes I'd sing the longest phrases,
And my voice would never tire.

Yet what always makes me wretched,
Is that I in silence pined,
For within my heart beloved,
You will always be enshrined.

Now I'm overcome with grieving,
As I sing my songs again,
I am filled with pain believing,
None is worthy of your name.

9. Frage

Wärst du nicht, heil'ger Abendschein!
Wärst du nicht, sternerhellte
  Nacht!
Du Blütenschmuck! Du üpp'ger Hain!
Und du, Gebirg' voll ernster Pracht!
Du Vogelsang aus Himmeln hoch!
Du Lied aus voller Menschenbrust,
Wärst du nicht, ach, was füllte
  noch
In arger Zeit ein Herz mit Lust?

9. Questions

Were you not there, holy evening light?
Were you not there, holy star bright
  night?
You gems of blooms, you shining bower,
And you great hills full of silent power.
You birds that sing from heaven above.
You songs that fill man's heart with love,
Without you, ah, what then would
  pacify
The hearts of troubled men?

10. Stille Tränen

Du bist vom Schlaf erstanden
Und wandelst durch die Au',
Da liegt ob allen Landen
Der Himmel wunderblau.

So lang du ohne Sorgen
Geschlummert schmerzenlos,
Der Himmel bis zum Morgen
Viel Tränen niedergoss.

In stillen Nächten weinet
Oft mancher aus den Schmerz,
Und morgens dann ihr meinet,
Stets fröhlich sei sein Herz.

Und morgens dann ihr meinet,
Stets fröhlich sei sein Herz.

10. Silent Tears

From slumber you have risen
The fields to wander through,
And to the far horizon
The sky is wondrous blue.

So long as you were sleeping
without pain, free from cares,
The heavens above were weeping,
And poured down endless tears.

In nights of silent grieving
Men's pain would be so great,
Next day you are believing
That gladness filled his heart.

Next day you are believing
That gladness filled his heart.

11. Wer machte dich so krank?

Dass du so krank geworden,
Wer hat es denn gemacht?
Kein kühler Hauch aus Norden
Und keine Sternennacht.

Kein Schatten unter Bäumen,
Nicht Glut des Sonnenstrahls,
Kein Schlummern und kein Träumen
Im Blütenbett des Tals.

Dass ich trag' Todeswunden,
Das ist der Menschen Tun;
Natur liess mich gesunden,
Sie lassen mich nicht ruhn.

11. What Made you so Ill?

Now that your pain is endless.
What brought about your plight?
Cold winter winds are blameless,
So is the starlit night.

No tree that gave you shelter,
Nor could the sun's warm rays,
Not dreaming and not slumber,
Nor flowers that bless your days.

That I am sick and ailing,
That is at man's behest,
Though Nature aids my healing,
They never let me rest.

12. Alte Laute

Hörst du den Vogel singen?
Siehst du den Blütenbaum?
Herz! kann dich das nicht bringen
Aus deinem bangen Traum?

Was hör' ich? alte Laute
Wehmüt'ger Jünglingsbrust,
Der Zeit, als ich vertraute
Der Welt und ihrer Lust.

Die Tage sind vergangen,
Mich heilt kein Kraut der Flur;
Und aus dem Traum, dem bangen,
Weckt mich ein Engel nur.

12. Old Sounds

Hear then how birds sing for you?
See then the trees in bloom?
Heart can this not restore you?
And end your dreams of doom.

Now I hear old songs bursting
Out of a young man's breast,
From times when I was trusting
The world, when we were blessed.

Those days are past returning,
No meadow root sustains.
Only an angel caring,
Can end my troubled dreams.

Robert Schumann

Liederkreis – Opus 39 (Eichendorf)

Composed 1840
   One cannot really call this Liederkreis a cycle, the songs are not related to one another and yet they share a unity since they are the work of a single poet, Eichendorff, and must not be confused with Liederkreis op 24 set to the poems of Heine.

Joseph Freiherr von Eichendorff.
   Born in Lubowitz in 1788 and died at Neisse, Silesia in 1857.
   Eichendorff was a central figure of the romantic movement, the writer of many poems with a strong feeling for the countryside and folk song.

1. In der Fremde

Aus der Heimat hinter den Blitzen
    rot
Da kommen die Wolken her,
Aber Vater und Mutter sind lange
    tot,
Es kennt mich dort keiner mehr.

Wie bald, ach wie bald kommt die stille
    Zeit,
Da ruhe ich auch, da ruhe ich auch und
    über mir
Rauscht die schöne Waldeinsamkeit,
die schöne Waldeinsamkeit,
Und keiner kennt mich mehr hier,
Und keiner kennt mich mehr hier.

1. Far from Home

From my distant home where the sky
    glows red,
The floating white clouds appear,
But my mother and father are long since
    dead,
And no one will know me there.

How soon, oh, how soon will that time
    draw nigh,
When I also rest, when I also rest, and
    over me sigh
The lovely trees where I lie?
The lovely trees where I lie,
And no one knows me here,
And no one knows me here.

2. Intermezzo

Dein Bildnis wunderselig
Hab' ich im Herzensgrund,
Das sieht so frisch und fröhlich
Mich an zu jeder Stund'.

Mein Herz still in sich singet
Ein altes, schönes Lied,
Das in die Luft sich schwinget
Und zu dir eilig zieht.

Dein Bildnis wunderselig
Hab' ich im Herzensgrund,
Das sieht so frisch und fröhlich
Mich an zu jeder, jeder Stund'.

2. Memory

Your image I hold tightly
Deep in my happy heart,
It looks at me so brightly
Each moment we're apart.

My heart softly is singing
A song of bygone days,
That through the air is winging
To you it swiftly flies.

Your image I hold tightly
Deep in my happy heart,
It looks at me so briskly
And every moment we're apart.

3. Waldesgespräch

Es ist schon spät, es ist schon kalt,
Was reit'st du einsam durch den Wald?
Der Wald ist lang, du bist allein,
Du schöne Braut! Ich führ' dich heim!

"Groß ist der Männer Trug und List,
Vor Schmerz mein Herz gebrochen ist,
Wohl irrt das Waldhorn her und hin,
O flieh! O flieh! Du weißt nicht, wer ich bin."

So reich geschmückt ist Roß und Weib,
So wunderschön, So wunderschön der junge Leib,
Jetzt kenn' ich dich—Gott steh' mir bei!
Du bist die Hexe Loreley.

"Du kennst mich wohl, Du kennst mich wohl von hohem Stein,
Schaut still mein Schloß tief in den Rhein.
Es ist schon spät, es ist schon kalt,
Kommst nimmermehr aus diesem Wald,
Nimmermehr, nimmermehr aus diesem Wald!"

3. Conversation in the Woods

It is so late, cold chills the blood,
Why ride you through this lonely wood?
The wood is vast, you are alone,
You lovely bride, I'll lead you home

Great is the guile and schemes of men,
With grief my heart is broken,
Bugles are calling far and near,
Oh flee, oh flee, my name you must not hear.

In gilt adorned is horse and bride,
So wonderful! so wonderful! Her form she cannot hide,
I know you now, God hear my cry!
You are the witch called Lorelei.

"You know me now, you know me now from steep incline,
My castle looks down on the Rhine.
It is so late, cold chills the blood,
You never more will leave this wood,
Never more, never will you leave this wood!"

4. Die Stille

Es weiß und rät es doch Keiner,
Wie mir so wohl ist, so wohl!
Ach, wüßt' es nur Einer, nur Einer,
Kein Mensch es sonst wissen soll!

So still ist's nicht draußen im Schnee,
So stumm und verschwiegen sind
Die Sterne nicht in der Höh',
Als meine Gedanken sind.

Ich wünscht', ich wär' ein Vöglein
Und zöge über das Meer,
Wohl über das Meer und weiter,
Bis daß ich im Himmel wär'!

Es weiß und rät es doch Keiner,
Wie mir so wohl ist, so wohl!
Ach, wüßt' es nur Einer, nur Einer,
Kein Mensch es sonst wissen sóll,
Kein Mensch es sonst wissen soll!

4. The Silence

No one can know or can guess it,
Why I'm aglow, all aglow!
To one only would I express it,
And no other person shall know!

The snow is so still where it lies,
So silent and secret are
The stars so high in the skies,
Less silent than my thoughts are.

I wish I was a swallow,
I'd fly right over the sea,
Yes, over the sea and further,
Then heaven my home would be.

No one can know or can guess it,
Why I'm aglow, all aglow!
To one only would I express it,
And no other person shall know,
And no-one will ever know!

5. Mondnacht

Es war, als hätt' der Himmel,
Die Erde still geküßt,
Daß sie im Blütenschimmer
Von ihm nur träumen müßt'.

Die Luft ging durch die Felder,
Die Ähren wogten sacht,
Es rauschten leis die Wälder,
So sternklar war die Nacht.

Und meine Seele spannte
Weit ihre Flügel aus,
Flog durch die stillen Lande,
Als flöge sie nach Haus.

5. Moonlit Sight

It was as if the heavens
Gave earth a silent kiss,
So earth in beauteous splendour
Would dream of heavenliness.

The breeze through cornfields playing,
To shake the ripening ears,
The treetops gently swaying,
The night sky bright with stars.

And my own soul is spreading
Its wings to freely roam,
Through silent land it's heading,
To fly me to my home.

6. Schöne Fremde

Es rauschen die Wipfel und schauern,
Als machten zu dieser Stund'
Um die halb versunkenen Mauern
Die alten Götter die Rund'.

Hier hinter den Myrtenbäumen
In heimlich dämmernder Pracht,
Was sprichst du wirr, wie in Träumen,
Zu mir, phantastische Nacht?

Es funkeln auf mich alle Sterne
Mit glühendem Liebesblick,
Es redet trunken die Ferne
Wie von künftigem großen Glück!

6. Distant Landscape

The treetops will quiver and rustle
As if at this very hour,
That around the half-ruined castle
The ancient Gods will appear.

Where branches of myrtle are swaying
In radiant fast fading light,
What then in dreams are you saying
To me, oh fantastic night?

The twinkling stars high above me,
With loving glances they shine,
They say in heaven how they love me,
And of joys that will soon be mine.

7. Auf einer Burg

Eingeschlafen auf der Lauer
Oben ist der alte Ritter;
Drüben gehen
   Regenschauer,
Und der Wald rauscht durch das Gitter.

Eingewachsen Bart und Haare,
Und versteinert Brust und Krause,
Sitzt er viele hundert Jahre
Oben in der stillen Klause.

Draußen ist es still und friedlich,
Alle sind in's Tal gezogen,
Waldesvögel einsam singen
In den leeren Fensterbogen.

Eine Hochzeit fährt da unten
Auf dem Rhein im Sonnenscheine,
Musikanten spielen munter,
Und die schöne Braut, die weinet.

7. In a Castle

High above within his towers
An old knight in death is waiting;
Darkening skies bring wind and
   showers,
And the trees beat on the grating.

Beard and hair have grown together,
Centuries a lonely tenant,
Petrified his breast and leather,
There he sits so still and silent.

Outside all is peace and quiet,
All have to the vale descended.
Birdsong through the window arches,
From the valley has ascended.

Far below a wedding party
On the sunlit Rhine is sailing,
Loudly play the gay musicians,
And the lovely bride is weeping.

8. In der Fremde

Ich hör' die Bächlein rauschen
Im Walde her und hin,
Im Walde, in dem Rauschen
Ich weiß nicht, wo ich bin.

Die Nachtigallen schlagen
Hier in der Einsamkeit,
Als wollten sie was sagen
Von der alten, schönen Zeit.

Die Mondesschimmer fliegen,
Als säh' ich unter mir
Das Schloß im Tale liegen,
Und ist doch so weit von hier!

Als müßte in dem Garten
Voll Rosen weiß und rot,
Meine Liebste auf mich warten,
Und ist doch so lange tot,
Und ist doch lange tot,
Und ist doch lange tot.

8. Away from Home

I hear the streamlets rushing
In woodlands all around,
In woods with all that rushing
I'm lost in all that sound.

The nightingales sing to me
Here in this lonely place,
As if they would remind me
Of the lovely bygone days.

Where moonbeams shimmer gaily,
I see there far below
A castle in the valley,
But it is too far to go.

A garden full of roses,
Full blooming, white and red,
Where my dear love reposes,
Yet she has been long since dead,
And she is long since dead,
And she is long since dead.

9. Wehmut

Ich kann wohl manchmal singen,
Als ob ich fröhlich sei,
Doch heimlich Tränen dringen,
Da wird das Herz mir frei.

Es lassen Nachtigallen,
Spielt draußen Frühlingsluft,
Der Sehnsucht Lied erschallen
Aus ihres Kerkers Gruft.

Da lauschen alle Herzen,
Und alles ist erfreut,
Doch keiner fühlt die Schmerzen,
Im Lied das tiefe Leid.

9. Melancholy

Sometimes a song disguises
My inward pain and grief,
A secret tear arises,
And brings my heart relief.

The springtime winds are playing,
Hear how nightingales engage
In mournful song betraying,
Such longing from their cage.

All hearts are filled with gladness,
Who hear them sing again,
Yet no one knows the sadness
That fill their songs with pain.

10. Zwielicht

Dämmrung will die Flügel spreiten,
Schaurig rühren sich die Bäume,
Wolken ziehn wie schwere Träume
Was will dieses Graun bedeuten?

Hast ein Reh du lieb vor andern,
Laß es nicht alleine grasen,
Jäger ziehn im Wald und blasen,
Stimmen hin und wieder wandern.

Hast du einen Freund hienieden,
Trau ihm nicht zu dieser Stunde,
Freundlich wohl mit Aug' und
    Munde,
Sinnt er Krieg im tück'schen Frieden.

Was heut gehet müde unter,
Hebt sich morgen neugeboren.
Manches geht in Nacht verloren
Hüte dich, sei wach und munter!

10. Twilight

Dusk on wings the wood is veiling,
Gruesomely the trees are stirring,
Clouds like heavy dreams are sailing,
What are all these signs foretelling?

If you have a deer you've cherished,
Let it not alone be grazing,
Nearby, huntsmen's horns are blazing,
Hear them calling through the forest.

If your friend begins to charm you,
Trust him not while it is twilight,
Smiles and eyes may show him
    forthright,
But with scheming he will harm you.

They that sink in rest so weary,
Rise new-born upon the morrow.
Many hopes are lost in sorrow,
Be on guard, alert and wary.

11. Im Walde

Es zog eine Hochzeit den Berg entlang,
Ich hörte die Vögel schlagen,
Da blitzten viel Reiter, das Waldhorn klang,
Das war ein lustiges Jagen!

Und eh' ich's gedacht, war alles verhallt,
Die Nacht bedecket die Runde;
Nur von den Bergen noch rauschet der Wald
Und mich schauert's im Herzensgrunde,
Und mich schauert's im Herzensgrunde.

11. In the Wood

A wedding procession passed down the vale,
I listened to birds all singing,
Then huntsmen, horns blaring, dash through the dale,
The chase its merriment bringing!

Before I could think, all faded away,
The night closed in all around me;
Now only trees on the hills creak and sway
As the dread in my heart surrounds me,
As the dread in my heart surrounds me.

12. Frühlingsnacht

Überm Garten durch die Lüfte
Hört' ich Wandervögel zieh'n,
Das bedeutet Frühlingsdüfte,
Unten fängt's schon an zu blühn.

Jauchzen möcht' ich, möchte weinen,
Ist mir's doch, als könnt's nicht sein!
Alte Wunder wieder scheinen
Mit dem Mondesglanz herein.

Und der Mond, die Sterne sagen's,
Und im Traume rauscht's der Hain
Und die Nachtigallen schlagen's:
Sie ist Deine, sie ist Dein!

12. Spring Night

See the swallows wheeling and diving
On warm breezes overhead,
That's the sign of spring arriving,
Flowers push upwards from their bed.

Shout with joy, I weep with pleasure,
Still to me I can't believe it quite!
Bygone wonders new to treasure
In the moon beam's golden light.

And the moon and stars are saying,
And the forest whispers its applause,
And the nightingales are crying,
She is yours, yes, she is yours.

Robert Schumann

Frauen-Liebe und Leben – A Woman's Love and Life

Frauen-Liebe und Leben (A Woman's Love and Life) is a cycle of poems by Adelbert von Chamisso, written in 1830. They trace the development of a woman's love and life with her man, from her perspective, from the moment of first meeting through marriage to his death, and after. Set to music as a song-cycle by Robert Schumann.

Schumann's choice of text was very probably inspired by events in his private life. He had been courting Clara Wieck, but her father had denied him permission to marry her. In 1840, after a lengthy and bitter legal battle, to make this permission no longer necessary, he eventually married her.

The songs of this cycle are noteworthy for the fact that the piano has a remarkable independence of voice. Breaking away from the Schubertian ideal, Schumann has the piano hold the mood of the song in its totality. Another significant feature is the circular structure of the cycle, in which the last movement repeats the theme of the first.

The songs were written two months before the Schumanns' wedding.

"One often hears that the poems of this cycle could be criticised as being old fashioned.

Perhaps for those people who live in the present day they are.

The sentimental way in which the maiden expresses her feelings are certainly not modern but is not love always a romantically exaggerated happiness or misery?

So, in this cycle let your mind be free to enjoy the romantic sentiment of a time which was far less matter of fact than our own".

Jeffrey Benton

1. Seit ich ihn gesehen

Seit ich ihn gesehen,
Glaub ich blind zu sein;
Wo ich hin nur blicke,
Seh ich ihn allein;
Wie im wachen Traume
Schwebt sein Bild mir vor,
Taucht aus tiefstem Dunkel,
Heller, heller nur empor.

Sonst ist licht und farblos
Alles um mich her,
Nach der Schwestern Spiele
Nicht begehr ich mehr,
Möchte lieber weinen,
Still im Kämmerlein;
Seit ich ihn gesehen,
Glaub ich blind zu sein.

1. When First I Saw Him

From the time I saw him,
He is on my mind;
Only him I'm seeing,
To all else I'm blind;
In a waking dreamland,
Floats his image on high,
Shining brightly, ever brighter,
In the deep blue sky.

Now all else has lost
Its colour and its shine,
For my sisters frolics,
I do not have time,
And in solitude I'm weeping,
To my room resigned;
From the moment I saw him,
To all else I'm blind.

2. Er, der Herrlichste von allen

Er, der Herrlichste von allen,
Wie so milde, wie so gut!
Holde Lippen, klares Auge,
Heller Sinn und fester Mut.

So wie dort in blauer Tiefe,
Hell und herrlich, jener Stern,
Also er an meinem Himmel,
Hell und herrlich, hehr und fern.

Wandle, wandle deine Bahnen;
Nur betrachten deinen Schein,
Nur in Demut ihn betrachten,
Selig nur und traurig sein!

Höre nicht mein stilles Beten,
Deinem Glücke nur geweiht;
Darfst mich niedre Magd nicht kennen,
Hoher Stern der Herrlichkeit,
Hoher Stern der Herrlichkeit!

Nur die Würdigste von allen
Darf beglücken deine Wahl,
Und ich will die Hohe segnen,
Viele tausendmal.

Will mich freuen dann und weinen,
Selig, selig bin ich dann;
Sollte mir das Herz auch brechen,
Brich, o Herz, was liegt daran?

Er, der Herrlichste von allen,
Wie so milde, wie so gut!
Holde Lippen, klares Auge,
Heller Sinn und fester Mut,
Wie so milde, wie so gut!

2. The Most Worthy of all Men

He most worthy of all men,
Oh so gentle and so kind!
Eyes the brightest, smile so charming,
Strong of heart and clear of mind.

He is there so high above me,
Glowing like a distant star,
He would be my own, my heaven,
Oh so close, and yet so far.

Go then, go where life will guide you,
I'll behold your glorious flight,
Meekly I will watch in sorrow,
Joy with pain is my delight.

Prayers I offer here in silence,
Given just for him alone,
He is far and high above me,
And to him I'll never be known,
And to him I'll not be known.

Only she who is most worthy,
Is your joyful happy choice,
And I'll give a thousand blessings
If in her you rejoice.

I'll give thanks in blissful sorrow,
Happy, happy I will be;
Even though my heart is breaking,
Break, oh heart and set me free.

He most worthy of all men,
Oh, so gentle and so kind,
Eyes the brightest, smile so charming,
Strong of heart and clear of mind,
Oh, so gentle, and so kind.

3. Ich kann's nicht fassen, nicht glauben

Ich kann's nicht fassen, nicht glauben,
Es hat ein Traum mich berückt;
Wie hätt er doch unter allen
Mich Arme erhöht und beglückt?

Mir war's, er habe gesprochen:
"Ich bin auf ewig dein"
Mir war's ich träume noch immer,
Es kann ja nimmer so sein
Es kann ja nimmer so sein.

O lass im Traume mich sterben,
Gewieget an seiner Brust,
Den seligen Tod mich schlürfen
In Tränen unendlicher Lust.

Ich kann's nicht fassen, nicht glauben,
Es hat ein Traum mich berückt;
Wie hätt er doch unter allen
Mich Arme erhöht und beglückt?
Ich kann's nicht fassen, nicht glauben,
Es hat ein Traum mich berückt;

3. My Wildest Dream

I could not ever believe it,
The dream I prayed for came true;
How could I among so many,
Poor me, has been blessed by you.

Was it to me he was speaking,
And said "always be mine"?
Will I be dreaming forever?
Do all dreams vanish with time?
Do all dreams vanish with time?

Oh let me die in my dreaming,
Held close in an endless kiss,
Then let me embrace my dying
While weeping in infinite bliss.

I could not ever believe it,
The dream I prayed for came true;
How could I among so many,
Poor me, has been chosen by you.
I still now cannot believe it,
The dream I prayed for came true.

4. Du Ring an meinem Finger

Du Ring an meinem Finger,
Mein goldenes Ringelein,
Ich drücke dich fromm an die Lippen,
Dich fromm an die Lippen, an
   das Herze mein.

Ich hatt ihn ausgeträumet,
Der Kindheit friedlich schönen Traum,
Ich fand allein mich, verloren
Im öden, unendlichen Raum.

Du Ring an meinem Finger
Da hast du mich erst belehrt,
Hast meinem Blick erschlossen
Des Lebens unendlichen, tiefen Wert.

Ich will ihm dienen, ihm leben,
Ihm angehören ganz,
Hin selber mich geben und finden
Verklärt mich, und findenverklärt mich
   in seinem Glanz.

Du Ring an meinem Finger,
Mein goldenes Ringelein,
Ich drücke dich fromm an die Lippen,
Dich fromm an die Lippen, an das
   Herze mein.

4. The Golden Ring

This ring upon my finger,
This golden ring I wear,
To my lips I will press you devoutly,
For my heart and my kiss, you will
   always be there.

I'm all alone and lost now,
This timeless, desolate, lonely place,
All lovely dreams of my childhood
Are lost in this infinite space.

Oh ring upon my finger
I see now what you mean,
My eyes have now been opened
To a vision of life that I've never seen.

From now I just wish to serve him,
To give to one so bold,
To be loyal to all of his wishes,
For him, and him only him, to
   have and to hold.

This ring upon my finger,
This golden ring I wear,
To my lips I will press you devoutly,
My heart and my kiss you will
   always share.

5. Helft mir, ihr Schwestern

Helft mir, ihr Schwestern, Freundlich mich schmücken,
Dient der Glücklichen heute mir,
Windet geschäftig Mir um die Stirne
Noch der blühenden Myrte Zier.

Als ich befriedigt, Freudigen Herzens,
Sonst dem Geliebten im Arme lag,
Immer noch rief er, Sehnsucht im Herzen,
Ungeduldig den heutigen Tag.

Helft mir, ihr Schwestern, Helft mir verscheuchen
Eine törichte Bangigkeit,
Dass ich mit klarem Aug ihn empfange,
Ihn, die Quelle der Freudigkeit.

Bist, mein Geliebter, Du mir erschienen,
Giebst du mir, Sonne, deinen Schein?
Lass mich in Andacht, Lass mich in Demut,
Lass mich verneigen dem Herren mein.

Streuet ihm, Schwestern, Streuet ihm Blumen,
Bringet ihm knospende Rosen dar,
Aber euch, Schwestern, Grüss ich mit Wehmut,
Freudig scheidend aus eurer Schar,
Freudig scheidend aus eurer Schar.

5. My Wedding Day

Help me my sisters, help me with dressing,
On this happy morning,
With lovely garlands busily weaving
Round my brow now adorning.

When in his arms with love I'm enfolded,
Soon will our joyful hearts unite,
Always he tells me of his own longing,
Waiting eager to share our delight.

Help me my sisters, help and distract me,
Help to banish my foolish fear,
That from the fountain of my own gladness,
I will go to him with eyes so clear.

When my beloved soon will be present,
Please let the sun shine brightly above,
Let me be faithful, Let me be humble,
Let me in graciousness show him my love.

Scatter his path with beautiful flowers,
Give to him roses to gladden his way,
But you, my sisters, show me your sadness,
As I leave you this joyous day,
As I leave you this joyous day.

6. Süsser Freund, du blickest

Süsser Freund, du blickest mich
 verwundert an,
Kannst es nicht begreifen, wie ich weinen
 kann;
Lass der feuchten Perlen ungewohnte
 Zier
Freudig hell erzittern in dem
 Auge mir!

Wie so bang mein Busen, wie so
 wonnevoll!
Wüsst ich nur mit Worten, wie ich's
 sagen soll;
Komm und birg dein Antlitz hier an
 meiner Brust,
Will in's Ohr dir flüstern alle
 meine Lust.

Weisst du nun die Tränen, die ich
 weinen kann,
Sollst du nicht sie sehen, du geliebter,
 geliebter Mann?
Bleib an meinem Herzen, fühle dessen
 Schlag,
Dass ich fest und fester nur dich
 drücken mag.
Fest und fester

Hier an meinem Bette hat die Wiege
 Raum,
Wo sie still verberge meinen holden
 Traum;
Kommen wird der Morgen, wo der
 Traum erwacht,
Und daraus dein Bildnis mir entgegen
 lacht.
Dein Bildnis

6. Tears of Joy

Dearest man why look at me
 enquiringly,
Can't you see my weeping is a
 gift from me?
Let the pearls of tears that fall show how
 I feel,
Eyes that brightly shine with love and joy
 so real.

Anxious is my heart, so full of
 joy today,
Wishing now I knew the words that
 I could say.
Come lay your head upon my
 breast to know,
While I softly whisper, why I
 love you so.

Hear my gentle sobbing, do you
 see my pain?
Why my heart is throbbing, you beloved,
 beloved man?
Ever closer hold me, Feel my beating
 heart,
With your arms enfold me close,
 never part,
Closer, closer.

Here beside my bed the cradle has its
 place,
Where I'll watch in wonder at the lovely
 face,
Soon will come the morning in a
 little while,
And my dream awakens with a winning
 smile,
You darling.

7. An meinem Herzen, an meiner Brust

An meinem Herzen, an meiner Brust,
Du meine Wonne, du meine Lust!
Das Glück ist die Liebe, die Lieb ist das Glück,
Ich hab's gesagt und nehm's nicht zurück.

Hab überschwenglich mich geschätzt,
Bin überglücklich aber jetzt.
Nur die da säugt, nur die da liebt
Das Kind, dem sie die Nahrung giebt;

Nur eine Mutter weiss allein,
Was lieben heisst und glücklich sein.
O, wie bedaur' ich doch den Mann,
Der Mutterglück nicht fühlen kann!

Du lieber, lieber Engel, Du
Du schauest mich an und lächelst dazu!
An meinem Herzen, an meiner Brust,
Du meine Wonne, du meine Lust!

7. A Mother's Love

Feeling your heartbeat, here through the night,
You are my pleasure, you my delight.
This bliss is what love is, and love is my bliss,
I will repeat and say only this.

The love I knew is in the past,
But now I've found true love at last.
Only to hold, only to feed my child
And give the milk it needs.

Only a nursing mother can feel
That loving joy that is so real.
For all of men I feel so sad,
From womans love this joy is made.

You look at me with smile so sweet,
My own darling child now life is complete,
Feeling your heartbeat, through the night,
You are my pleasure and my delight.

8. Nun hast du mir den ersten Schmerz getan

Nun hast du mir den ersten Schmerz getan,
Der aber traf.
Du schläfst, du harter, unbarmherz'ger Mann,
Den Todesschlaf.

Es blicket die Verlassne vor sich hin,
Die Welt ist leer, ist leer.
Geliebet hab ich und gelebt,
Ich bin nicht lebend mehr.

Ich zieh mich in mein Innres still zurück,
Der Schleier fällt,
Da hab ich dich und mein verlornes Glück,
Du meine Welt!

8. Lost Happiness

Now for the first time you have caused me pain,
That pain of death.
You sleep my man, never to take again,
Another breath.

I cannot see the world, what is life for?
And I'm alone, alone.
So loved I was and so alive,
But now I live no more.

Behind the veil my visions still remain,
Forever held,
And there I see lost happiness and pain,
You are my world.

Mahler

Lieder eines fahrenden Gesellen – Songs of a Wayfarer

Mahler's *Lieder eines fahrenden Gesellen* covers a wide range of emotions through unorthodox tonality, falling fourths and so on. One might say that this wayfaring lad is a nephew of the wanderer in Schubert's *Winterreise*. Both wayfarers were forsaken by their loved ones which plunged them into despair. In Mahler's case the cycle re-echoes his unhappy love affair with the actress Johanne Richter. Furthermore, unlike the cycles of Beethoven, Schubert and Schumann, the poems were written by Mahler himself.

In the first song the cheerful music which will enliven the wedding party soon takes on a gloomy atmosphere as the dejected lover tries to console himself with the beauties of nature by imitating the song of the birds as does young Siegfried in Wagner's opera of that name. But there is a sense of grief in the soft-footed piano accompaniment which brings into reality this self-deception.

The steady rhythm in the piano part of the next song, which fluctuates between staccato and legato, seems to say that for the moment the youth is happy to share in spring's jubilation. In the last line of the song we come to realise that his yearning is all in vein.

The fortissimo chords which herald in the voice in an outburst of despair in the following song has a suicidal ring to it.

Here, the agony is so unbearable it seems as if a dagger has been plunged into his breast. His cries of bitter resentment to the pain that never rests is mirrored in the piano part.

In the last, and most beautiful of the songs, the blue eyes of the young girl are the only consolation as the traveller sets out on his lonely journey with love and sorrow as his only companions. The tranquil movement of the song is akin to the 'Brook's Lullaby' with which Schubert brings his cycle *Die schöne Müllerin* to a close.

© *Philip Rodden*

1. Wenn mein Schatz Hochzeit macht

Wenn mein Schatz Hochzeit macht,
Fröhliche Hochzeit macht,
Hab' ich meinen traurigen Tag!
Geh' ich in mein Kämmerlein,
Dunkles Kämmerlein!
Weine! wein'! Um meinen Schatz,
Um meinen lieben Schatz!

Blümlein blau! Blümlein blau!
Verdorre nicht! Verdorre nicht!
Vöglein süß! Vöglein süß!
Du singst auf grüner Heide!
Ach, wie ist die Welt so schön!
Ziküth! Ziküth!

Singet nicht! Blühet nicht!
Lenz ist ja vorbei!
Alles Singen ist nun aus!
Des Abends, wenn ich schlafen geh',
Denk' ich an mein Leid!
An mein Leide!

1. On my Sweetheart's Wedding Day

On my sweetheart's wedding day,
merry will the wedding be.
It will be my saddest day.
To my gloomy little room,
dark and gloomy little room,
weeping, weeping for my love,
for my dearest love.

Frail blue flower, Frail blue flower,
0 wither not, 0 wither not;
Little bird sing so sweet,
you sing on green heathland.
Ah, this is a world so fair.
Chirrah! Chirrah!

Sing no more, bloom no more,
Spring is over now,
Every song is over now.
When evening comes I try to sleep,
thinking of my sorrow,
of my sorrow.

2. Ging heut' Morgen über's Feld

Ging heut' morgen über's Feld,
Tau noch auf den Gräsern hing;
Sprach zu mir der lust'ge Fink:
"Ei du! Gelt?
Guten Morgen! Ei, Gelt? Du!
Wird's nicht eine schöne Welt?
schöne Welt?
Zink! Zink! Schön und flink!
Wie mir doch die Welt gefällt!"

Auch die Glockenblum' am Feld
Hat mir lustig, guter Ding',
Mit den Glöckchen, klinge, kling,
klinge, kling,
Ihren Morgengruß geschellt:
"Wird's nicht eine schöne Welt?
schöne Welt?
Kling! Kling! Kling! Kling!
Schönes Ding!
Wie mir doch die Welt gefällt!
Heiah!"

Und da fing im Sonnenschein
Gleich die Welt zu funkeln an;
Alles, alles, Ton und Farbe gewann!
Im Sonnenschein!
Blum' und Vogel, groß und klein!
"Guten Tag! Guten Tag!
Ist's nicht eine schöne Welt?
Ei, du! Gelt? Ei, du! Gelt?
Schöne Welt!"

Nun fängt auch mein Glück wohl an?
Nun fängt auch mein Glück wohl an?
Nein! Nein! Das ich mein',
Mir nimmer, nimmer blühen kann!

2. Walking in the Fields Today

Walking in the fields today
dew still on the grasses hung,
spoke to me the merry finch:
"Hey you there!
Hey, good morning, hey you there,
is it not a lovely, lovely world?
lovely world?
Sing, sing lovely and bright.
Ah, how much I love the world."

And the harebell in the field,
in her happy spirit sings
and her tiny bells will ring,
faintly ring.
Hear her morning greetings ring.
"Is it not a lovely, lovely world?
Lovely world?
Ding, ding, ding, ding,
lovely thing.
Ah, how much I love the world.
Heigh, ho!"

Now the sun is shining bright,
fills the world with sparkling light.
All then, all has gained its brightest hue,
in sunshine,
birds and flowers great and small.
"Lovely day, Lovely day,
is it not a lovely world?
Hey you there, hey you there,
lovely world!"

Will my joy return once more?
Will my joy return once more?
Oh no, I well know.
That it will never bloom again.

3. Ich hab' ein glühend Messer

Ich hab' ein glühend Messer,
Ein Messer in meiner Brust,
O weh! O weh!
Das schneid't so tief
In jede Freud' und jede Lust,
So tief! so tief!
Es schneid't so weh und tief!

Ach, was ist das für ein böser Gast!
Ach, was ist das für ein böser Gast!
Nimmer hält er Ruh',
Nimmer hält er Rast!
Nicht bei Tag,
Nicht bei Nacht, wenn ich schlief!
O weh! O weh! O weh!
O weh!

Wenn ich in dem Himmel seh',
Seh' ich zwei blaue Augen steh'n!
O weh! O weh!
Wenn ich im gelben Felde geh',
Seh' ich von fern das blonde Haar
Im Winde wehn! O weh! O weh!
Wenn ich aus dem Traum auffahr'
Und höre klingen ihr silbern Lachen,
O weh! O weh!
Ich wollt', ich läg' auf der schwarzen Bahr',
Könnt' nimmer, nimmer die Augen aufmachen!

3. I have a Burning Dagger

I have a burning dagger,
a dagger deep in my heart,
Ah pain, such pain
it cuts so deep.
In every joy and pleasure deep,
so deep, so deep
it cuts with pain so deep.

Ah, why must I have this evil guest?
Ah, why must I have this evil guest?
never is he hushed,
never will he rest.
Not by day,
not by night when I sleep.
Ah pain, Ah pain.
Ah pain.

When I look into the sky,
there I can see the bluest eyes.
Ah pain, Ah pain.
When in the golden fields I roam,
there I can see her golden hair
on breezes blown. Ah pain, ah pain.
And when from my dream I start
then I hear laughter, her silver laughter,
Ah pain, Ah pain.
I wish I lay in the darkest
    grave.
Oh never, never to waken
    again.

4. Die zwei blauen Augen von meinem Schatz

Die zwei blauen Augen von meinem
    Schatz,
Die haben mich in die weite Welt
    geschickt.
Da mußt' ich Abschied nehmen
    vom
Allerliebsten Platz!
O Augen blau, warum habt ihr mich
    angeblickt?
Nun hab' ich ewig Leid und Grämen!

Ich bin ausgegangen in stiller
    Nacht,
In stiller Nacht,
Wohl über die dunkle
    Heide.
Hat mir niemand Ade gesagt, Ade!
Ade! Ade!
Mein Gesell' war Lieb' und Leide!

Auf der Straße stand ein Lindenbaum,
Da hab' ich zum ersten Mal im Schlaf
    geruht!
Unter dem Lindenbaum,
Der hat seine Blüten über mich
    geschneit,
Da wußt' ich nicht, wie das Leben tut,
War alles, alles wieder gut!
Ach, alles wieder gut!
Alles! Alles!
Lieb und Leid,
und Welt und Traum!

4. These Two Blue Eyes

Those two bluest of eyes of my dear
    love.
They now have sent me away into the
    world.
So I must say farewell now, and leave
    this
dearest place.
O eyes of blue, why did you gaze at me
    with love?
Now all I ever know is pain and grieving.

I must leave this place now in still of
    night,
in stillest night,
In the darkness I go through the
    heathland.
Is there no one to say farewell, farewell,
farewell, farewell,
my companion is love, is love and grief.

By the roadside stands a linden tree,
I rested at last within its
    shadow.
Under the linden tree,
it's branches have showered me with
    blossoms white.
I then forgot what life can do,
and all was well, was well once more.
Ah, all was well once more.
All, all,
love and grief,
the world and dreams.

Alexander von Fielitz

Eliland – Song Of Chiemsee

I hold the theory that no composer has ever had a vogue in his day without having done something to deserve it.

When rummaging through dusty old scores by some nigh forgotten composers one sometimes comes across the odd Edelstein such as Alexander von Fielitz's song cycle Eliland.

A contemporary of Hugo Wolf and Brahms, (1860 – 1930), Alexander von Fielitz studied composition with Edmund Kretschmer and piano with the Czech virtuoso Schulhoff – a protege of Chopin – in Dresden. He wrote piano pieces and two operas which were staged throughout Germany.

He worked with Nikisch and conducted in the USA and at the Theatre des Westerns in Berlin where Caruso appeared as a guest in 1906. He also held teaching posts in Chicago and at the prestigious Berlin Sternscher Singakademie.

His fame as a composer rests mainly on his song output especially his settings of Eichendorf, von Gilm, Lenau, and the ten Kaspar Stieler poems which constitute the Eliland cycle.

Stieler (1632-7707) was a prolific writer of verse much of which has religious undertones, two of his poems are to be found in the Penguin book of Lieder.

The songs of von Fielitz were popular fare with many great

concert singers at the turn of the century including such giants of Lieder singing as the tenor Raimund von zur-Mühlen and the baritone Ludwig Wüllner. The latter used to sing regularly at the Sunday Evening Mennigen Concerts at which he, accompanied by Brahms, sang Lieder by the Master.

In the Eliland songs we detect in von Fielitz's style a cross section between Grieg and Schumann discernible in such songs as *Heimliche Grüße*, and *Kinderslimmen*.

Eliland would be worthy for inclusion in any recital programme by those singers ever in search of the unusual. Blomberg's Victorian English translation of 1902, is greatly superseded here by Jeffrey Benton.

© *Philip Rodden*

1. Stilles Leid

Eine stille Zelle
An blauer Welle,
Das ist mein Leid.
Wohlan, ich trag' es,
Aber ich klag' es
Doch allezeit!

Ich hab' mein Leben
An Gott gegeben,
Und das ist sein.
Das wend' ich nimmer,
Doch denk' ich immer:
O, wär' es mein!
O, wär' es mein!

1. Silent Grief

In my cell so silent
by the cool blue water,
sorrow is mine.
So well sustaining,
always complaining,
yes, all the time.

My life is given
to God in heaven
to him alone.
I'll turn not ever
my life is never.
never my own.
Oh, never my own.

2. Frauenwörth

Das war ein Tag voll
   Maienwind,
Da ist auf blauen Wogen
Zu Nonnenwörth ein Grafenkind
Gar lenzhold eingezogen.

Die war geheißen Irmingard;
Ich sah es, wie der Bangen
Kränzlein und Schleier eigen ward
Die Nonnen alle sangen.

Ihr aber fielen die Tränen drauf,
Die barg ich lang im Sinne;
Nun gingen sie mir im Herzen auf
Als Knospen süßer Minne.

2. The Convent

Spring came at last with May winds
   mild,
I gazed across the water.
The convent took a nobleman child
to take her last vows they brought her.

Her name is Irmingard, they said,
I saw her doubt and misgiving.
Garlands and veil adorned her head
and all the nuns were singing.

But her distress she could not conceal
my tears were overflowing;
and in my heart, my beating heart
the bud of sweet love was growing.

3. Rosenzweige

Wohl manchen Rosenzweig brach ich vom Pfade
Am grünen Strand,
Es trug der Wind ihn fort an ihr Gestade,
Bis sie ihn fand.

Sie flocht den Kranz sich draus
zum Kirchengange
O holde Noth!
Von meinen Rosen ward ihr Stirn und Wange
So heiß und roth!

3. Roses

So many roses red, for her I gathered
down by the shore.
The breezes sent my flowers across the water,
she found them all.

She made a garland,
at church she wore it;
Ah sweet distress
from my red roses on her cheeks,
so shyly the blushes caress.

4. Heimliche Grüsse

O Irmingard, wie schön bist du,
Holdseliger ist keine;
Bei grünen Linden wandelst du
Im luftigen Sonnenscheine!

O Irmingard, wie silbern klingt
Dein Sang zu uns herüber;
Wie fliegen meine Grüße
    beschwingt
In euer Gärtlein hinüber!

Wie zage Vöglein bergen sie sich
Im tiefen Gezweig der Linden,
Doch wenn du wandelst und denkst an
    mich,
Magst du sie drinnen finden!

O Irmingard, wie schön bist du.

4. Secret Greetings

Oh Irmingard how fair you are,
no one ever could be sweeter.
Beneath the linden tree she walks,
the sun brightly shines to greet her.

O Irmingard like silver bells,
your song to me is ringing.
On wings of love to your garden from
    here
my greetings so tender are bringing.

So shyly the songbirds hide in the trees,
so deep in the boughs above her.
So as you walk and you think of
    me
will they our love discover.

Oh Irmingard my fairest love.

5. Am Strande

Mein Liebling ist ein Lindenbaum,
Der steht am Strand;
Es spielen die Wogen mit leisem
 Schaum
Um den weißen Sand.

Und der Lindenduft, der zieht mir
 hinein
Bis ins tiefste Gemüt,
Halt still, mein Herze, und gib dich
 drein,
Du hast geblüht!

5. Along the Shore

My favourite trees, the Lindens grow
along the strand,
and playfully waves gently ebb and
 flow
on the silver sand.

And the linden flowers invade my
 mind
with fragrant perfume
be still my heart your fate
 resigned,
why did love bloom?

6. Kinderstimmen

Mit unsern Fischern war ein Kind
   gekommen
Von Frauenwörth.
Das hab' ich spielend auf mein Knie
   genommen
Und frug betört:

"Wer ist die lieblichste der frommen
   Frauen,
Die du gewahrt?"
Da schlug es auf den vollen Blick, den
   blauen:
"Frau Irmingard!"

6. Child Voices

With our returning
   fishermen
a boy came to us one day,
I called to him and on my knee I took
   him.
and said in play

'Of all the nuns my son, who is the
   fairest
in your regard?'
With glance so sharp, his eyes so blue
   and certain
'It's Irmingard.'

7. Mondnacht

Ich lieg' an meines Lagers End'
Und lug' in stille Sterne;
Die blaue Woge, die uns trennt,
Wie rauscht sie leis und ferne!

Verschleiert schaut der Mond herein,
Mein Herz hält stille Feier;
Wie sind so bleich die Wangen dein,
Wie ist so dicht dein Schleier!

7. The Moonlight

I watch the silent starry skies
while on my bed I'm lying,
the lake so blue between us lies
it's waves are faintly sighing.

A cloud conceals the moon from sight
my heart has no more feeling
Oh Irmingard your cheeks so white
how closely drawn your veiling.

8. Wanderträume

O, der Alpen blanke Kette,
Wie sie glänzt im Morgenblau!
Daß ich dort mein Wandern hätte,
Wenn im Wald noch liegt der Tau,

Langgelockt und freigelassen,
Wie ich's einst gewesen bin, –
Scharfe Pfeile möcht' ich fassen;
Singend zög' ich dort dahin,

Wo am tiefsten niederhinge
Das Gezweig auf meine Fahrt –
Und an meiner Seite ginge
Schleierlos Frau Irmingard!

8. Dreams

See the alps, the mountain ranges
how they shine in morning light,
that I there might still now wander,
when the woods are dewy bright,

Oh to be there free forever,
as I once was long ago.
Sharpened arrows in my quiver,
sing and tarry here and there,

where the hanging branches hide me
through the woods and in the dale,
and with Irmingard beside me.
Roaming free without her veil.

9. Anathema

Nun ist wohl Sanges Ende!
Wie hart ich davon schied',
Die Wintersunnenwende
Ist kommen für mein Lied!

Es rief der Abt mit Zürnen
Mich in die Zelle sein
Und sprach: "Dein Herz sei hürnen
Und deine Gedanken rein!

Was heimlich du geschrieben,
Mir ward es offenbart;
Fluch über dein sündig Lieben,
Fluch über Frau Irmingard!

Doch eh' der Tag zerfallen,
Das schwör' mir zu Gesicht:
Sei von den Liedern allen
Nicht eines mehr am Licht!"

9. Denounced

Now all my songs are ended,
how hard it is to part.
The winter has returned now,
for songs that filled my heart.

The abbot called in anger
and to his cell I'm brought.
He spoke "Thy heart should ever
be of the purest thought.

The secret songs you've written
are in the open now,
cursed be thy sinful loving,
a curse be on Irmingard.

Before this day, is over
then swear before my sight,
of all thy secret love songs
not one will see the light!"

10. Ergebung

Gehorchen ist das erste!
Ich hab' mich stumm geneigt,
Und ob das Herz mir berste,
Mein Herz gehorcht und schweigt.

Mich hat mein Abt verfluchet,
Ich war wohl gottverwaist,
Daß Sang mir heimgesuchet
So süß den stillen Geist!

Euch Lieder aber trag' ich
Zum walt in stiller Fahrt,
Und letzte Grüße sag' ich
Nun dir, Frau Irmingard!

Dort will ich in Waldgrund legen
Sie unter eisernem Schrein
Und ihre Hüter mögen
Waldvöglein, die lieben, sein!

Und mag sie je ergründen
Ein Pilger auf seinem Pfad,
So bin ich ohne Sünden,
Ein Mönch, dem Gott genad'.

10. Resignation

Obedience is my duty
and I must silence keep,
and though my heart is breaking
of love it must not speak.

My abbot has accused me
that I had God defied
I searched my heart for love songs
so sweet to soothe my mind

My songs I now must carry
to woodlands' quiet shade,
and send my last fond greeting
to you my Irmingard.

There in the woods I'll hide them
an iron casket their tomb,
to be protected fondly
by the birds where she loved to roam.

And if a wandering pilgrim
discovers the hiding place,
am I then free from sinning?
a monk who fell from grace.

ACKNOWLEDGEMENTS

With much gratitude

To my wife Dorothy, to whom I could always rely on for support, and my children, Andrew, Sadieann and Jonathan.

To Jonathan for putting together this book, for corrections and formatting.

*To Derek Hammond-Stroud OBE
and
Philip Rodden
For their contributions and advice*

*And to Simon Taylor
Portrait Painter.*

About the Author

Jeffrey Benton is a singer whose musicianship, dramatic communication and feeling for words, distinguish him amongst the finest of baritones. Jeffrey was based in London for much of his career and has played leading roles in many West End productions, notably 'The Great Waltz' and 'Gone with the Wind' at Drury Lane, and 'Showboat' at The Adelphi. He has also appeared in a Royal Variety Performance at the Palladium and sung in opera and operetta on television, as well as giving many recitals of classical music at the Wigmore Hall and at the West Bank.

His numerous Lieder recitals at the Wigmore Hall, South Bank, and Leighton House have led to high critical acclaim.

After studying music and singing at the Guildhall School of Music, Jeffrey was given invaluable guidance in vocal technique by Derek Hammond-Stroud O.B.E.

Jeffrey has a particular interest in translating Lieder into English. His recordings in this field include Schubert's 'Winterreise' (Symposium 1118) and 'Die Schöne Müllerin' (Exegete 0011), Schumann's 'Dichterliebe' (Symposium 1221), Beethoven's 'An Die Ferne Geliebte' (Symposium 1221), Mahler's 'Lieder Eines Fahrenden Gesellen' (Symposium 1221) and Von Fielitz' 'Eliland' (Symposium 1119). All in his own translations.

To record Winterreise in English had been a burning ambition for many years.

After performing it many times in it's original language, Jeffrey knew it was perfect for translation. An ongoing study of the work, together with a youthful experience (whilst serving with the Grenadier Guards in Germany) of similar proportion to that of the young poet of Muller's work, brings a fresh insight to 'The Winter Journey'. He has endeavoured to show that, as the cycle progresses, the bewildered young man at the start becomes more bitter and disillusioned as his journey takes him away from all that he loves.

His love of English Song is equally important. 'If Doughty Deeds' (Symposium 1159) celebrated the 150th anniversary of the birth of Sir Arthur Sullivan and includes some of the composer's lesser known songs and piano pieces.

Roger Quilter songs are among his elected favourites and Volume 1 (Symposium 1159) includes a premier compact disc recording of the Arnold Book of Old Songs. Volume 2 (Symposium 1184) is a premier recording of all the Shakespeare settings.

Jeffrey has also recorded 'The Old English Melodies' (Exegete 0012) arranged by Henry Lane Wilson, and until then less than a third of the songs which constitute the collection had been recorded. This is the first complete recording.

Jeffrey is the only singer to have recorded Schubert's Winterreise both in its original language and also in his own English translation.